COTTON EVERYWHERE

RECOLLECTIONS OF NORTHERN WOMEN MILLWORKERS

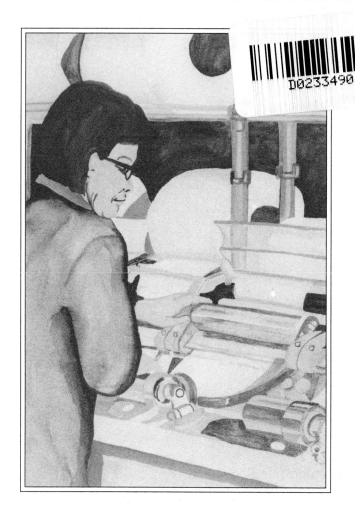

Written and Illustrated
by Christine Kenny

AURORA
Publishing

© Aurora Publishing 1994
Aurora Enterprises Limited
Unit 9, Bradley Fold Trading Estate,
Radcliffe Moor Road, Bradley Fold,
Bolton BL2 6RT.
Tel: 0204–370752

ISBN 1 85926 037 3

Written and illustrated by: Christine Kenny
Edited by: Dawn Robinson-Walsh

Cover Picture: *A Spinning Machine*

Origination, printed and bound by:
Manchester Free Press
Longford Trading Estate,
Thomas Street, Stretford,
Manchester M32 0JT.
Tel: 061–864 4540

FOREWORDS

Bolton, so evocatively conjured up by the oral-history accounts lovingly presented by Christine Kenny in this book, is both totally familiar and almost completely foreign to me. Like many of the women whose voices speak in *Cotton Everywhere*, Bolton — *my* Bolton, *their* Bolton — is the Bolton of *then*, the 1930s and 40s and 50s, rather than of *now*, the 1990s. However, there is an important, indeed, a crucial difference here between my Bolton and theirs.

The women that Christine interviewed in order to prepare *Cotton Everywhere* speak about their experiences *in* Bolton (family life, childhood, working in the mills, war, marriage), and also their experiences *of* Bolton (its dialect, its local foods, its traditional forms of labour). These experiences are direct ones, the experiences that have composed their lives, all the many hours and days that together make 'a life' and its memories. My experience, ostensibly of the 'same' Bolton over the same time period, is a very different one; for it comes, not from my own memory, from any lived experience, but instead from accounts produced at the same time and stored within the Bolton (or 'Worktown') part of the Mass-Observation Archive at the University of Sussex. Mass-observation studied everyday life of everyday working-class people from the 1930s to the early 1950s, from all over Britain, not just Bolton. However, for many people — perhaps especially Boltonians, of course! — it is the 'Worktown' part of Mass-Observation's work that is the most memorable, even though this forms only a relatively small part of a very much larger archive.

Mass-Observation's 'Worktown' is composed by the accounts of the researchers and students who came to Bolton, or who were Boltonians themselves, in the form of detailed written accounts (as well as the, perhaps, better-known photographs that are a part of this Archive, taken by Humphrey Spender, and some of which can be seen locally). These accounts were written up from reports of everyday events – the Mass-Observers did not 'interview' or 'survey'; they were instead interested in observing life as it was naturally occurring around them. 'My Bolton', as I have referred to it, is one pieced-together from now many years' research on the Mass-Observation Archive more generally, and which is in a way superimposed on the Bolton of today of 'then' that is much more real to me and which I trace out the remains of somehow 'beneath' the new roads, shopping areas and the like.

My Bolton, then, is a very real one for me; it exists clearly in my mind, in words, but also in photographs and newsclips. It is a clear, but essentially emotionless place in my mind. This is very different indeed from the Bolton of the women whose memories compose *Cotton Everywhere*, for theirs is a Bolton composed of memories, sweet and bitter, still pungent. *Their* Bolton is one shaped, burnished bright and illuminated by these acts of memory provided for readers through the transcribed 'voices' we hear in these pages. Christine Kenny writes a little about the problems with memory as an oral-history resource, that it can sometimes distort and omit because memory always has limits (even when we do not know what these limits are).

Quite rightly, she chooses, instead, to stress the 'story-telling' of the women whose memories and voices she relies upon, and its power to evoke, even for those of us who, like most readers of this book, will not have 'been there' ourselves. Memory has limits; but let us not forget that so too do all other ways of researching social life, in the present as well as the past. We should also not forget that memory has an enormous strength, one which gives it a great advantage over other research approaches, because only memory based upon direct experience has the power to make readers feel that they can almost smell the same smells, almost hear the same sounds, almost feel the same feelings.

This is exactly what make *Cotton Everywhere* such a very good read. It may not make the past 'live again', but it does the next best thing by enabling us to hear the voices of women who lived it then, and who now remember it so clearly and so evocatively

Dr. Liz Stanley
Reader in Sociology, University of Manchester

This book is a collection of personal reminiscences and conversations which took place in the late 1980s with women from the working class of Lancashire whose life-experiences encompass the span of the twentieth century. It gives the reader an insightful record of the vast social changes that have taken place in that time, but also identifies the unchanging indomitability of the human spirit. Although the commentators are women, there is a noticeable absence of bitterness or hostility towards men, but there is a ready appreciation of the difficulties with which both the sexes had to deal, often in a supportive partnership.

Ms Kenny writes in an open, self-confident style, and is in complete empathy with the women and their lives. One senses the trust between the participants in the conversations over a range of what one might describe as the central life experiences — work, romance, health, home-life and earliest childhood memories, war and peace. The reminiscences are realistic, humorous and tender. The reader is made aware of the continuity of many aspects of women's experience when Ms Kenny contributes her own early memories which are those of a later generation. This is a fascinating book which provides the reader with fresh insights each time it is taken up. A book to keep and treasure!

Dr. Laverne Pearson
Lecturer in Educational Psychology, Bolton Institute

This book is a lively, and at times moving, addition to the growing literature of oral history. The motivation for this type of history writing is to 'tell it like it was' or, as it is sometimes called, 'history from the bottom up'. This history is written, not by the winners, but by those whose lives were shaped and given meaning by everyday experiences.

The women in this book have at last found a voice with which to communicate to others outside their immediate world of workmates, family and neighbourhood, They tell of universal female experiences, courtship, childbirth, bereavement and working lives which nevertheless remain unique to them.

The most remarkable point to emerge is the very 'normality' of women working outside the home. The women here rarely questioned their place in the public world of waged work and it is important that this be recognised today. Too often it is assumed that women in the recent past were all content to take their 'natural place' as housewives and full-time mothers and this sets the record straight. Like the author, I too was brought up in a world where women worked and, although this was set in a West London suburb, I recognised many similarities with my own childhood.

Certain vivid pictures of a community which was organised around work, which are evoked in this book, remain in the memory. I am thinking particularly of the description of the noise of the tramp of marching feet, and of front doors slamming, to which it was a part of childhood to be awoken by in the early morning. This is especially poignant when it is remembered that this scene was still being enacted as recently as the 1950s, and has now completely disappeared.

This book recreates a world in which not only was it normal for women to work, but that their work itself was a source of interest and a firm base in people's lives. Work in the cotton mills was obviously hard, dirty and exhausting; but it gave people a sense of pride and an identity, as well as locking them into a whole structure of friendships and social networks.

The description of 'the night they bombed Manchester' is one of the most vivid I have read of the blitz. Stripped of romanticism and nostalgia, it is an account of ordinary people surviving in extraordinary situations.

The women speaking here do not romanticise the past, they do not talk of the 'good old days', but they contribute to our understanding of what it was like to 'be there'.

Dr. Anthea Symonds
University of Wales, Swansea

GRATEFUL THANKS

My thanks to the following women for taking part in the study:–

My late Grandmother, Elsie Miller

My late Aunty Lily

My great Aunty Gladys Stevens

My great Aunty Sarah Ann Daubney

My Mother, Joan Miller

Mrs. Alice Best

Mrs. Alice Bryan

The late Mrs. Annie Lane

Mrs. Florence Lomax

Mrs. Hilda Peace Unsworth

Mrs. Bessy Winstanley

The remaining women expressed a wish that
their names should not be mentioned

CONTENTS

ACKNOWLEDGMENTS

It seems appropriate to begin by acknowledging my parents, extended family and the people of the community in which I grew up (many of whom contributed to the material gathered for this book). These people did much to shape my early experience and development. Thank you all for your love, your care and most of all, your stories. I would also like to thank Erica Burman and Sue Wilkinson for giving me the confidence and encouragement to write the book in the first place and finally Alec Bagley and Phil Goodman, my academic critics and friends for their help and advice.

INTRODUCTION

This book evolved from a series of interviews I conducted with 14 Bolton women, all of whom spent their working lives in the cotton mills. The stories focus almost exclusively on women's experiences of the mills. While it is recognised that men also worked in the textile industry, I am of the view that women's history generally has been neglected and this has created a gap which needs to be filled. This book therefore attempts to redress this imbalance in a small way. The stories are woven very much in my own life and experience. Many of the women in my family and community in which I grew up worked in the mills (I also worked in one for a short span of time). Because of this my understanding of the mills was partly formed long before I conducted these interviews.

The women of the community in which I grew up were interesting and lively storytellers — I loved to listen to them as a child. Hopefully, the readers of this book will find the stories as fascinating as I once did (and still do). These storytellers had a profound influence on my development as a child and did much to shape the adult that I am today. Conducting the interviews therefore, was an interesting experience for me because as each woman told her story, she provoked in me the replay of dusty memories stored in the furthest regions of my mind. The mills of Bolton spun cotton — and a fabric of cultural experience, thinking and values. This book in turn, has been woven from a warp and weft of narrative and memory which will hopefully act as a catalyst bringing to the fore some sense of nostalgia to those who read it.

The retirement party of Eileen Gorse, including Irene Martin, Jean Hill, Mr. Priestley, Eileen Gorse, Frances Denton, Betty Isherwood, Ann Lathem and Nora.

My thanks to Mr. Priestley who was very kind to me when I worked in the mill and did much to encourage my painting and drawing.

The stories in the book are not necessarily completely accurate because they are based on memory, which has the ability to distort and omit. It is also difficult to pinpoint exactly when some of the events described happened, since when people remember their lives they rarely do so in a strict chronological order. There is much literature available nowadays which provides factual information about the mills but this book attempts to give the reader some insight into how people actually felt about them (from the early part of this century to more recent times) about their private lives in connection with them and of their experience of the two Wars.

If any number of people witness the same event, they will experience it differently because we are all individuals. Because of this, those who read this book who have experienced similar events to those described in it, may say 'well it wasn't like that for me,' and it probably wasn't. In this book I do not claim to be giving a story of all Bolton people, rather I give the stories of some of them and I also give some of my own. This is because Bolton has shaped my life and experience and this has been woven into the threads of the fabric during the interviews. I have known all but four of the women who took part in this study for most of my life and I felt that I could not and should not separate my experience from theirs.

My academic background is that of a psychologist but I have tried to avoid wrapping the experiences of the women I have interviewed around some complicated academic theory because I want to invite the reader to interpret the stories as much as possible, in his or her own way. I give an 'open text.' Thus members of the academic community are free to intellectualise the stories within the framework of their own discipline, while those outside academia have the freedom to develop a few theories of their own. I feel the reader should remember however, that the people I interviewed have given us a valuable part of themselves. So theorise as much as you want, but remember to treat the yarn of this fabric with some respect.

My intention in writing these stories (mine and the women I interviewed) was to use our experience as the raw materials to create something which is interesting and a pleasurable experience to read. I wanted this book to go beyond description, I wanted it to engage in a conversation with you, the reader. As you read the stories, I hope you will find yourself saying to yourself, 'oh yes, I remember that.' The memories which inhabit this text, form part of Bolton's cultural heritage and this belongs to the people of Bolton (although it hoped that others may also find it to be of interest).

Christine Kenny

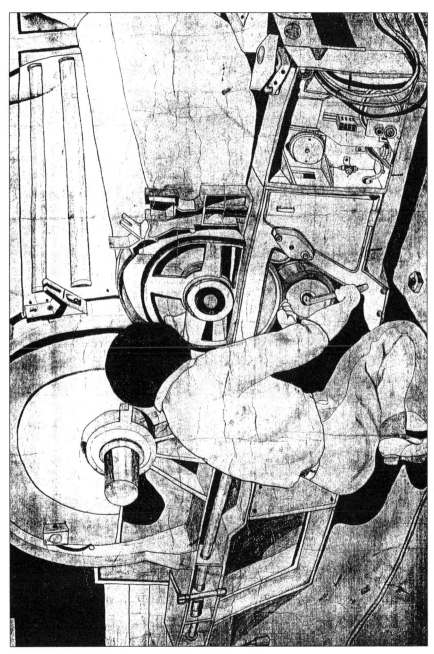

Working on a Carding Machine.

CHAPTER ONE

THE KNOCKER UPPER

One of my earliest childhood memories is of early morning darkness. As I dozily approached the exit of sleepy land, I remember a sharp tapping on our bedroom window. I must have been very young then and my bed or cot must have been situated near the front bedroom window. The sound certainly seemed very near, a curious blending of phonetics, tin and glass, shocking me into consciousness — the tapping, and its accompanying set of feet, 'clip, clop' making their impact on the pavement as their owner continued up the street. Tap, tap, clip, clop, welcoming sounds to a young child, indicating the commencement of another day, another chance to immerse oneself in this new experience — life. Some mornings the tapping would be followed by a brief exchange, bad language and polite insistence. The workers didn't want this Monday morning and the knocker up's reputation depended on the ability to awaken reluctant sleepers. This conflict of interest made itself evident with an amusing verbal exchange which was to always end with the victory of the knocker upper.

I remember the bliss of lying in a warm cot, hearing the muffled sounds of a parent dressing to meet the day — a tired parent who had been denied sleep by a much livelier me the night before. And then the sound of an approaching army, distant at first but gathering momentum as front doors slammed and more and more people joined the march — people on their way to work. Eventually the noise became so loud that it denied anyone the luxury of a semi conscious state and I would then lean over the cot to look outside from the bedroom window into the street.

In this way I could observe the march, the parade of God knows how many workers' heads passing my window. Oh boy! Adults must be so important to be involved in this. No wonder they are so BIG!

The experience was short, lasting about an hour after which the march had moved on into the unknown. The street returned to a temporary silence broken only by the isolated, hurried tapping of the occasional late worker who had refused earlier to succumb to the charms of the knocker upper. Slowly, day descended on the street.

The knocker upper disappeared from Bolton life and my memory assigned the file to the back of the filing cabinet, until I started my interviews. Then one of the interviewees mentioned the knocker upper and the file burst open onto the desktop of my mind. But who was the knocker upper? In my childhood memory this was an invisible person, his presence only evidenced by his pole, the sound of his feet and his occasional reply to an angry worker.

I had always tended to think the knocker upper was male but it seems from my interviews that this was an occupation open to both men and women. The important thing was a strong sense of self enterprise, an ability to get up early and to spot an open opportunity. The sound created by the knocker upper, similar to beads falling on glass, proved to be a bit of a mystery — how was it made? I realised that no ordinary stick could create such a sound. Indeed, a stick might well have shattered the glass. Few of the women interviewed in this study had any idea what the knocker upper's stick was like; they seemed surprised to have been asked. Everyone in the study however, remembered its characteristic sound.

❖ *When I was a girl there was an old couple used to do it. They used to come at five o' clock in the morning and they used to have a long stick with wires on the end. They used to come in at the back. Where we lived, everyone had a front parlour, at the front — that was your fancy place like . . . and she'd come in and bang on the window with these wires. She'd shout, 'Come on now, it's five o'clock.' They only cost you a few coppers but they did a lot and it built up. A lot employed them because no one*

would have got up without them. The alarm clock probably
wouldn't have got you up and then most people couldn't afford
alarm clocks, they were an expense then, but yes she used to
make a living wage, her and her husband — but they had to get
up early . . . oh, I remember the knocker upper coming, she was a
nice old lady. All the areas had a knocker upper, it was a way of
life having a knocker upper.

Part of Bolton life or not, it surprised me to find that very few of the women interviewed ever saw theirs, or even knew who it was knocking on their window every morning. But as my interviewees pointed out, most people were asleep when the knocker upper called. Therefore it was only the adult of the house who was responsible for hiring and paying the knocker upper who ever came into contact with them. For many people in Bolton the knocker upper was a faceless person.

❖ — *It was just a man who came round and knocked people up.*
I don't know who paid him, but we used to be frightened to
death of being late.

Discussions of the knocker upper during the interviews had a knock on effect. Memories of them conjured up images of the early morning march which had once been so characteristic of Bolton life. The storyteller quoted below for example, vividly remembered the uniform clogs, shawls and black stockings of the early mill workers.

❖ — *Yes, I used to have one here, it was five shillings a*
week . . . he'd knock us up at five o'clock . . . then on his way up
he'd see if you were up and if you weren't he'd give you another
knock . . . but my early recollection was of people going to work
in clogs . . . well, when I went to work, they didn't wear clogs —
well, you could if you wanted to — but it was shoes then, rather
than clogs, so you didn't get the clatter on the cobble stones like
you used to do when I was little . . . I have worn clogs when I
was little, blue ones and black ones, but I couldn't stand the
clatter of them, I had rubbers put on them so that it nulled them

*a bit, but they always used to be heavy on my feet and I caught
my ankle on them . . . so I gave over wearing them for that
reason. In my childhood of course they used to have the shawl
and black stockings going to work, now it's coats and everything
that's fancy.*

Many of the women remembered the march as a social event. As
worker joined worker, a network system of local news was set into
operation and everyone genned* themselves up with the latest events. For
a short period of my life, I remember these early morning discussions as
I walked to work with my mother. The walk was refreshing (unless of
course, it happened to be foggy) because workers caught the day in its
best clothes — dawn and in winter, the fresh smell of drying rain. My
mother and I called this smell 'Christmas' because it was most frequently
in the air around late November, early December. At this time of the year,
Christmas tree lights shone from the windows of homes and shops adding
·enchantment to the morning and cheering the hearts of workers as they
plodded to their place of employment. Some of the women remembered
this early morning smell when they talked of the workers daily march.

❖ *It was nice at that time in the morning, there was a nice smell.*

Do you remember that reader — the smell of Christmas? Of course
you do. Maybe you didn't call it that but there was a special smell to those
early mornings, maybe we still have it. I wouldn't know, since I'm no
longer up and walking the streets at the early hour of seven a.m.

Knocking up could not have been an easy job. It seems from the
accounts that there was a lot of walking to do because a patch could be
quite long. A reliable knocker upper took the work very seriously. Their
good reputation depended on getting people up, no matter how difficult
this might be and they would frequently knock again on their journey back
down the patch if they noticed that a household was still unlit. The
knocker upper's determination to get everyone on the patch up gave the

---

* *Genned up is a Bolton term meaning to get up to date with the latest gossip.*

service a human touch that the (then) expensive alarm clocks could not compete with.

> ❖ — *They didn't all have alarm clocks then for a long time like they do now. You know a really good alarm clock, a reliable one could cost you a lot of money, they could be very dear, and you couldn't rely on your clocks like you could on your knocker upper, and he wouldn't go away until you got up you know and knocked on the window to show you were up (laughs). Some did get a swear at if the workers were half asleep you know, I mean not everyone's well mannered when they first wake up are they?*

We take alarm clocks so much for granted in the nineties that it is hard to imagine that many people once could not afford them. But the older storytellers could remember a time when an alarm clock had been considered a very advanced piece of technology and a luxury few people could afford. The alarm clock is one example of how technology has changed peoples' lives radically in the course of the 20th century. Televisions, washing machines, 'phones and a host of other household items are considered by no means exceptional items in peoples' homes in the nineties — yet all were once viewed with awe and amazement. With regard to the alarm clock, these are now cheap, convenient and widely available. When we consider it, the alarm clock is a wonderful and convenient addition to any home but like so many other technological advances, alarm clocks have caused unemployment. No one has a knocker upper any more and what a pity. There are so many unemployed people nowadays who could provide themselves with a useful occupation knocking up in the same way that others have done in the past. However, the knocker upper's patch was protected in the past in the same way in which window cleaning rounds and the like are today.

> ❖ *They had to wait for a vacancy, it was like window cleaning today, you know how window cleaners have their own patch . . . well, they couldn't move in and take someone's patch and all the knocker uppers kept to their patch.*

So, the knocker uppers like other respectable business people, kept to their patch. It would be quite wrong to assume (as I once did) that anyone could set themselves up as a knocker upper. Anyone wishing to take up this occupation had to wait for a vacancy and once a patch was established it was protected, 'owned,' by the knocker upper.

The knocker uppers also had to face many of the potential threats and frustrations experienced by early morning workers today, such as the post man.

❖ *We used to have a dog and she wouldn't bite anyone normally, we kept her in the yard . . . but if she had pups we had to take her in the house because she went for the knocker upper once, so they had all that to put up with as well.*

It came as a pleasant surprise, during my interviews to find that the father of one of the women had been a knocker upper. This man became a knocker upper after he had been made redundant from his job and this was to remain his occupation until his retirement.

❖ *— Shall I tell you what my father did? Well, I've never been ashamed to say it, but he was a knocker upper . . . I went on my holidays two year since, I met a man there, he said, 'I like the people of Bolton,' he said, 'there was a man there who used to come and knock us up.' He said, 'he was lively, he used to say, "come on its raining" and all this,' and I laughed to myself and I said, 'that was my Dad.' I'm never ashamed of admitting that's what he did because he did that rather than have no money and he made a living wage out of it, and how he come to do it was, his aunty used to do it, she used to knock a few up and when she was poorly he took it up until she died. They all kept saying, 'will you knock us up as well?' So his patch grew, and he used to get up at 4 o'clock in the morning, and he made a living wage knocking up. Well, he had no dole or anything, you see in them days they didn't have dole . . . I can't remember how much he used to charge now. 2p, 4p, it was only coppers, and he used to*

go back and give them another knock. He wasn't frightened of
that, oh they all knew him my Dad, yes he was a lively character.
He was a lively man.

This storyteller remembered much of her father's activities during his career as a knocker upper but even she was not sure about the type of stick used. She explained that as far as she could remember her father's stick had been a long piece of bamboo which flipped backwards and forwards on the window without causing the glass to shatter. But she added that the type of stick used varied. Some sticks she said, may have had wire on the top although she couldn't say for sure.

The knocker upper appears to have a long history in Bolton. Everyone interviewed remembered having one. But no-one knew for sure how or when knocking up started, not even the older women interviewed. However, a few offered some possible explanations.

❖ *People didn't have dole then, you see, so they had to make*
money as best way they could. If people couldn't get work then
they had to make work ... I suppose someone must have been out
of work sometime and they must have thought about doing that
and well I suppose it caught on like ideas do, don't they? When
people see a good idea well it catches on, but no I can't tell you
who started it, I mean, I'm like you, I can remember having a
knocker upper when I was a little girl and I'm in my eighties, so
they must have been around a long time.

By the time I was born however, the age of the knocker upper was coming to an end. When I asked my mother about the one we had when I was small, it seems he was one of the few left. My maternal grandmother had not, at least as far as my mother remembered, employed the services of a knocker upper, so that being knocked up in the mornings once she married was a new experience for her. When my parents married and moved to the home of my early childhood, Lyons Street, there were so few knocker uppers left that if your area was covered by one then you were considered to be very lucky.

❖ — *Oh, yes, we had a knocker upper, in the next street.*
I believe he was one of the very last knocker uppers in Bolton,
and he was very reliable . . . and Dad had to get up very early
because he had a fresh job, he was a lorry driver and he had to
get to the docks, so this meant he had to be up at five o' clock.
Now the knocker upper used to come around about six o' clock.
There was two mornings a week he had to go to the dock early
(my father) so he said to him, 'you've no need to come around on
such a morning and such a morning because I'm going to the
docks,' so he said, (the knocker upper) 'does that mean you have
to get up earlier,' and he said, 'yes,' so he said, 'well, I'll come
around and knock you up,' and he did that, he did us this very
special favour of coming to knock an hour earlier so that Dad
would get up in time for the docks.'

So it seems that right to the end the knocker uppers took their work
seriously and if necessary went out of their way to ensure that they
provided a good service. But what caused the decline of the knocker
upper? The answer was much simpler than I thought.

❖ — *People bought alarm clocks you see. Alarm clocks got*
cheaper and more people could afford them . . . so I suppose that
were it.

So it would appear that the homely, human, almost vulnerable tap-
tap of the knocker upper (supremely effective though it was) was made
extinct by this mechanical, unforgiving, relentless clang of modern technology. But there is one question I have failed in my research to answer
— who knocked up the knocker upper?

CHAPTER TWO

TIPPING UP YOUR DREAMS

I'm stood in the middle of the street, Lyons Street, the little cobbled back to back street where I began my life. It's been raining and the wet of the pavement is seeping into my sandals. The smell of Christmas is in the air and I *was* feeling really proud because I've just pointed my dad out to a friend. Can you see that man over there? The one leaning on that big lorry smoking a fag — well that's my dad. He drives that lorry all by himself, that's what he does for a job, that's his work. He's also handsome, the neighbours told me. I'm not really sure what this 'handsome' is, but I know it's something to be proud of, you know how adults have all these things that they think are important? Well, handsome is one of them. That's why I like to point him out to my friends, especially those friends whose dads don't have any handsome — then I can feel really smug.

It would have been a really nice day but the adults have spoiled it. All the adults are at their front doors making recommendations. Yes I should have my hair cut. Yes it was unruly and yes it would, like my mother said, grow even longer and stronger if I had it cut. Grown ups are like that. It's not as if you've just got your mum to cope with. Oh no! Family business is street business. Oh well, I'll have it cut. Then I can have it longer then ever. I'll show them.

See! I told you! I had my hair cut yesterday. They said it would grow longer if I did — longer and thicker. That was a downright fib. It's still short this morning. Adults — you've got to be cute to deal with them. They tell you off about fibbing and they do it all the time. But they are

25

clever about it. They lie by omission, fail to give the 'true facts.'

Provided you handled them carefully though, grown ups could be OK. And I suppose they must be important because they work. Work — now that's the place where adults go when you don't see them around. Work — behind the word was a nothingness for me at this time in my life. My mind did not concern itself with conjuring up any image of what work might be like. I had no real conception of what it was. Work was a tag which explained the absence of adults and nothing more. I did not even associate the very visible presence of the mills with work because it was outside my level of awareness. Work — the privileged secret world of adults.

I knew that one day I would work, and I knew exactly what I would be — a lady astronaut. My parents had bought an impressive new telly and I had become hooked on the programme, 'Lost in Space.' The characters in the programme wore nice smart outfits. Much nicer than the tatty overalls speckled with cotton worn by the adults of my world. So it was decided, I would be a lady astronaut so that I could wear a nice outfit and fly around in space. I discussed my career prospects with the adults and these were taken seriously. If I worked hard at school I could be whatever I wanted to be. And as the adults so rightly pointed out, lady astronauts were very important — they were needed to cook the fellas teas.

Children's career prospects were taken seriously (it seemed then) and never ridiculed by the adults of my childhood world. Why shouldn't children enjoy a little fantasy? Adulthood and all its responsibilities came soon enough. And of course, encouragement was provided for those children whose future career required early practice. My mother had no qualms about giving my brother her best baking tray so that he could prepare for his future career as a cowboy — by eating beans from a tin plate.

But dreams are dreams and they are totally disconnected from reality, as many of the storytellers pointed out. For generations of adults in Bolton who came before me (and many who came after) the road to adulthood took only one course, the local mills. For my generation, educational opportunities were beginning to open up. But the adults of my childhood world had few choices open to them, although they had all enjoyed their own dreams and aspirations as children. Quite a number of the storytellers reported having early ambitions to go into nursing but these aspirations were never fulfilled. The failure to have their childhood dreams realised, led to some feeling disappointed and dissatisfied with their jobs in the mill. Most of the storytellers remembered their first impressions of the mill vividly. On the whole, these memories were very negative.

> ❖ *I didn't like it because I didn't want to go in the mill in the first place. I actually wanted to go into nursing but I didn't have the qualifications, and you had to buy your own books and uniform . . . well we just couldn't afford it, so my Grandad and Grandma who had brought me up put me in the mill . . . you know there's a saying in Bolton 'I'll put you through the mill,' and that's where it comes from, the mill.*

When discussing their earlier ambitions, most of the women spoke of them as little more than dreams.

> ❖ *I always wanted to do nursing when the War was on, but it was only day dreams wasn't it, things like that? Well, I was stuck in the mill and that's where I stayed . . . and they used to say, 'she's not going in the mill' (parents) and all this, but there was no jobs, unless you went working in Woolworth's or something. For such as our level, we couldn't get jobs, they wouldn't entertain you, you see without qualifications; of course those with more education got the better jobs.*

It is clear from some of the things which were said during the interviews, that some parents did not wish for their children to go into the mills. But it seems that there was a lack of knowledge amongst parents about the education system as well as a lack of opportunities.

> ❖ *— I don't think the adults took enough interest in that, they had no money. I mean if you passed (for grammar school) that*

was one thing, but when it came to paying they couldn't afford
it so they never gave it a second thought, it was the uniform and
all that and the books, they couldn't afford it so they never gave
it a second thought.

Families were poor and the wage of a young adult was a useful
(indeed sometimes necessary) addition to the family budget. If children
went into Further or Higher education then parents would have to sacrifice money the young person could be bringing into the home. In addition, parents would have to pay for books, equipment, uniforms — all
of which could have crippled the family financially. Some of the storytellers came from families who had wanted to avoid sending children to
work in the mills. Such parents had apparently insisted that their son/
daughter would have educational opportunities made available to them.
But when it came to the crunch, the storytellers in my study did not
succeed any better than their contemporaries. Poverty, the unpredictability
of employment trends which led to frequent breaks and dependence on
the dole, meant that the parents never did collect the nest egg which would
keep their child out of the mill.

The majority of women interviewed in this study learned to bury their
sense of disappointment of failing to have their dreams realised and they
began to experience the mill in much more positive ways, although this
was by no means true of them all. Some felt extremely bitter about their
working lives in the mills.

❖ — *I am bitter about it love, I always have been Christine, I'm*
bitter about it because I couldn't do the job a wanted to do in the
first place . . . I don't know (if others felt bitter) because most
people fully expected to go in the mill, but I fully expected to go
and be a nurse and they wouldn't let me and I was put in the
mill and I didn't want to go in. I used to lose my temper quite a
lot at work, least thing got my temper up because I didn't like the
job . . . everything, I detested everything, there wasn't anything
about the mills that I liked. It was hard work, it was a chore to
get up and go; in fact, quite a few mornings I cried because I had

to go, I cracked up because I didn't want to go and it was even worse if you got up and a few things had gone wrong, and a couple of times I've come home at dinner and I've not gone back in the afternoon. I couldn't face it you see love, I hated it, I really hated it.

Few of the women who took part in the study talked of choosing to go in the mill, people were put there. The storytellers spoke of how the mill made them hard and toughened them up. Use of such terminology may reflect the hard work of the mill and also the lack of control and personal choice which most of the women in the study experienced in their lives, and indeed the lack of choice for parents.

Once a young person left school there was an added incentive for parents to get them a job, any job, even a job in the mill — the dole school. The dole school was mentioned by the older women but not by those in their late fifties. So it can be assumed that the dole school had been dispensed with by the 1950s. If a young person was unable to find work prior to this, attendance at the dole school was compulsory. It seems from what the storytellers have said, that there was a stigma attached to attending the dole school. The father of one of the storytellers had been particularly insistent that his daughter would not spend her working life in the mill. But when she reached adulthood this same father was actively seeking work for her in the mills so that she could avoid the stigma of having attended the dole school.

❖ — *Well, we weren't working very long before they stopped us and then you had to go to the dole school, you had to go to school if you weren't working till you found a job, I think they stopped it shortly after that (early 1950s) but my Dad said 'you're not going to that dole school' Well, you didn't want to go there, it was nothing to be proud of, you know, so my Dad got me on at one of the local mills.*

It must have been hard for these parents to see the dreams they had fostered for their children dissolve over the years (unless of course they coped by forgetting that they had ever had such aspirations). Parents don't change. We all hope for a better life for our children and try to protect them from repeating our mistakes, experiencing our disappointments and faded dreams. There are perhaps better educational opportunities available to people of different social backgrounds in the nineties — a few. But for the parents of the women in this study hoping for Further or Higher education for their child seemed like asking for the moon. For the women in the study in their late eighties at the time of interview, introduction to the mills began before they had left school.

> ❖ — *Well, before you went to work full time, you started first in the afternoon, you went half time, you started in the mill at morning, then we had to run all the way home for our dinner, then we went on to school in the afternoon. We started work when we were 14, so we'd be about 13.*

Only one of the storytellers interviewed, knew of a young person of her cohort who had managed to get to grammar school and this was an only child whose father had been lucky enough to remain in unbroken employment until the boy grew up.

> ❖ — *Yes, one lad who lived at the end of the street . . . he was an only child though, there was just him, so his parents could afford it, the books and all that, and his dad had a good job . . . so, yes, he went to grammar school.*

But even the dreams of these parents were to be lost, as the storyteller explained.

> ❖ — *He was a prisoner of war after he was called up (in the Second World War, this woman is in her seventies) . . . it must have been a terrible experience . . . he was never the same after he came back. Oh, it was terrible, the war, there were some nice lads killed from round here, and even when they did come back there were some terrible problems.*

There is another story in this book dealing with the effects of the War. The writer considered it important however, to draw attention to the various factors, including the war experiences which channelled the working class people of Bolton towards employment in the mills. The mill was so much a part of adult life in Bolton that two of the storytellers admitted to never having considered anything else. Both of the storytellers were women in their eighties when interviewed. This older group did appear to have a greater acceptance of mill life than did the younger sample (women under the age of seventy). The older women did have their dreams and many reported them. But whereas the other storytellers all described their dreams during the interview, these two women did not. There are two possible explanations for this. The first is that the two women never had any dreams. This is possible because the women who reported dreams, did so without invitation when asked about how they felt about going in the mill, or when asked to describe their first impressions of it. Dreams and aspirations were always given prior to descriptions of the mill. It was as if the storytellers were putting forward an image of their wished for self, before their actual, lived self. The second explanation is that these two women had enjoyed their dreams in childhood but had considered them unrealistic so many years ago, that they had forgotten them. Judging from the way the two women talked about the mills, it seems more likely that their lack of dream reporting came about because they simply never had any. It seems from what the women said that they already felt strongly connected to the mills long before they ever set foot in one.

❖ — *Well, my mother worked in the mill and I had an idea what it was like when I heard my mother talk and I knew more or less everyone worked in the mill because there wasn't much industry; yes, I liked it.*

For the second woman who failed to report dreams, her family's traditional connection with the textile unions seems to have drawn her to the mill. This woman was to become very active in the union later in her adult life, so that union and the textile industry were seen by her to be closely connected.

> ❖ — *I had been brought up in a trade union household because my mother worked in the local card room, my father worked at the local sewage works and both were connected to the union and so I didn't really get any peace until I joined the union.*

This storyteller involved herself in the union activities from an early age, albeit at a basic level at the beginning by collecting the workers' contributions and taking these to the Spinner's Hall (Bolton's meeting place for trades union affairs). However this early involvement was to lead for her into an interesting career in the unions, a topic which is covered in greater depth in chapter six.

Regardless of whether the women had dreamed of an alternative career to that of going in the mill or not, most of them spoke of their first impressions in a very negative way.

> ***Chris*** — *when you first went working in the mill, what were your first impressions of it?*

> ❖ — *Well, it was awful, because going straight from school like that, it was a bit overwhelming for a child at 14. Today they have a bit better idea of what to expect, we were innocent in those days . . . it was frightening really for a child I thought and I was terribly shy because I'd just lost my mother prior to that.*

Another storyteller when asked how she felt the very first time she entered the mill said:

> ❖ — *The noise, the feeling of 'let me get out of here', the feeling that I wanted to walk through one door and find another to get out, there was the noise, the heat although it wasn't as hot in the winding room as it was in the spinning and card room, but I felt that the machines themselves, took a long time for me to get used to them.*

This feeling of being overwhelmed was reported by almost all the storytellers including the women in their eighties who had began working part time whilst still at school. Interestingly, however, this older group did not labour on the topic as much as the younger women.

❖ — *Noisy, it was noisy and hot. Oh, heck, I remember that.*

Noise and heat were the discomforts reported the most when the storytellers discussed their early impressions of the mill. Yet much to my surprise no one mentioned the smell of the cotton itself. I had worked in the mill for a short period as a young woman (I was 16 at the time) and for me the most noticeable characteristic of the mill was the strong smell of cotton. The smell of cotton is an 'acquired taste,' as the saying goes. I found it extremely heavy and unpleasant at first, but as the months went on, it became a similar smell which I associated with a familiar place. We have a textile department at Bolton Institute where I now work as a lecturer. I have walked through the textile department on a number of occasions and I have purposefully inhaled deeply in order to maximise my sensation of this odour which experience taught me to enjoy. The smell of cotton is unlike anything else I have experienced, so that I cannot adequately describe it, except to say that it is 'heavy'. Maybe the women in this study worked with the smell for so long that they had stopped noticing it, or maybe they noticed it but took it so much for granted that they didn't consider it worthy of a mention.

Once the women had been working in the mills for a period of time, it is clear that they began to enjoy themselves. Many of the storytellers spoke with affection of older women who had been their superiors who, in addition to training the younger girls, took a custodial role.

❖ — *The older women were respected, you looked up to them and in addition to training you on the job, they also educated you about life.*

But some of these older women took the role of disciplinarian a little too far.

❖ — *Oh, they were rat bags! Oh, yes! I worked with one and she was only little, she was the old-fashioned mill type, black stockings and clogs and if you didn't do something straight away she'd knock you to it.*

Chris — *Do you mean hit you?*

❖ — *No, I mean push you.*

It seems the young adults could be vulnerable if the older women under whose supervision they worked misused the power that they had. The actual work of young adults entering the mill seems to have been very monotonous and dirty at first. Young people entering the mill did not have a machine for which they were responsible (called in mill jargon, having a side of your own). Most young people worked in teams, doing the more basic and repetitive jobs such as setting on (putting the bobbins in place ready for piecing up) cleaning the machines or doffing. Cleaning in the early days of this century must have been a very dirty and dangerous job because it often meant crawling under the machines, getting covered in dirt and oil in the process, to clean intricate parts of the machine. That such work was dangerous is suggested by reports of accidents or of close encounters with a potential accident, given by the women themselves.

Chris — *Was it dangerous working with that kind of machinery, were there any accidents?*

❖ — *A lot of danger because there was no covers over or anything. I once nearly, well I was very lucky because they had these great big straps going over the carding machines and they used to have brushes, long brushes to clean them, well we had to clean our machines, and one day I was cleaning this machine and it went around the strap and I must have shouted out, I must have screamed out and the carder, they called them that — the boss, I mean — came running and then fortunately it didn't break or anything, so I was very lucky.*

The issue of safety is to be more fully covered in chapter three. I have raised the issue in this chapter in connection with early experience, in order to point out that work in the mill was much more than a sacrifice of dreams, it was very dangerous for young and old alike. The accidents were reported exclusively by those women in their seventies and eighties, so it seems that work safety was improving over the years. But when it is considered how much we protect our young people around the ages of 13 and 14, it really seems quite shocking that our forebears were exposed to such dangers. One of the woman reported the death of one of her cousins in the mill, a young man.

❖ — *Oh, yes, I had a cousin, me mother's brother's lad, he was a little piecer, but he got killed in a Spinning Mule. There were poles in the building coming from the ceiling and he must have got near the poles to walk with the machine, going backwards and forwards, he was only young, and he got twisted me mother said, he got twisted round and he died. I can't remember exactly how old he was, but he was very young.*

Once people started working in the mill, ambition was all about getting a side of your own. Once you got your own side you had it made, more interesting work, power (as much as the storytellers ever had anyway) and better pay. By the time workers acquired their own side, it seems from the interviews, that they had become settled in the culture and ways of life in the mills.

❖ — *I enjoyed working as a winder because I could daydream. I enjoyed daydreaming and once I picked up those scissors to start knotting, I was automatic apart from anything else . . . but I could leave that winding room anytime I wanted and dream of all the things I wanted to do, or could do if I worked hard enough . . . but in those days you were expected to tip up your wage, every penny, and this was common, and when you tipped your wage up you had to depend on the generosity of a parent, so that the amount of money people had varied anything from five shillings to one pound, I was in the five shilling range (both laugh).*

You see reader? Working class people don't necessarily give up their dreams once they start work. Some of the women who took part in my study, reported the ways in which they would replay their dreams during the day. One advantage of having a repetitive job is that it allows you the luxury of dreaming. How many workers today hate their jobs, but cannot enjoy the escapism of daydreaming, because their work demands *just enough* concentration to prevent it. But dreams exist in peoples heads. Real life for the storytellers who took part in this study, was tipping up your dreams, along with your wages at the end of every working week.

CHAPTER THREE

VICTORIAN VALUES

In the last chapter it was stressed that the storytellers who took part in this study had few options open to them other than that of working in the mill. Many had talked of their feelings of disappointment because they had missed various opportunities. But others had positive as well as negative feelings about the mills once they got used to working in them. For some, the positive feelings by far outweighed the negative. Negative memories of working in the mills included the long hours and the poor working environments. Positive aspects included the wages, pride in the work and friendship — this last being reported the most frequently of all. For married women, the mills provided some respite from the home and financial independence. The storytellers had mixed opinions about the wages they received as mill workers. On the one hand, when compared to other occupations open to women the wages were quite good. But when the long hours and hard physical work were taken into account then the pay seemed quite low.

Conditions with regard to the health and safety of employees did improve over the years although change was slow. The older storytellers who had witnessed the implementation of change considered that the working environment in the mills in late sixties and early seventies were quite good. The younger storytellers however, did not think that the improvements had been good enough.

The conditions of the mills in the early part of this century, described by the older women were horrendous — dirty and unsafe. There were inadequate facilities for workers to attend to their personal hygiene, and washing had to be done in a single bucket of water shared by all the workers in each department, and this was rarely, if ever, changed during the day.

❖ *You used to wash yourself in a bucket . . . that were when
I first started, but as years went by, it came as they put wash
basins on the landings, and you could go and wash you, and
they supplied us with towels, but they didn't supply you with
towels when I first started, you had to take your own.
Everyone used to rush to be the first to wash their hands in't
bucket because if you'd been doing oily jobs and you had a
wash well, everyone had to wash in that bucket . . . and if you
were last, well it would be full of oil.*

In addition to the job they were employed to do, workers were also responsible for cleaning the machines on which they worked. This was a filthy task, no doubt all the more unpleasant for the older women in the early mills because of the inadequate washing facilities. It was the new-comers to the mill, young people around the age of 14 who were often responsible for the dirtiest cleaning work. The storytellers quoted below recall their experiences of working in the mill when they were 14 years old.

❖ *It were dirty, because you had to get on the floor all the time,
and it got all your clean pinnies dirty because you were down in
all the muck and grease and oil and that, and they switched
machines off, and then you had to get down under the machine,
and clean all the muck off the machines.*

❖ *You used to sit on't floor, on't greasy floor to do what they
called the frame feet, so what we used to do, we used to get long
strips that our mothers had done with and put them on, and tie
a piece of binding round, and then we used to sit on't floor and
you slided yourself along while you stopped the machine and you
slid yourself along while you cleaned the frame feet and*

*underneath with a brush and a wiper and you got rid of all the
dust and wiped all the oil up and that once a week, and you had
all your other jobs to do as well, it did your back that did.*

Working in the mills was hot — hot and uncomfortable. The younger storytellers commented on the heat and they at least enjoyed the advantage of wearing shorter briefer clothing when they had worked. For the older women it must have been unbearable. The men who worked in the mills could at least get some relief from the heat by simply stripping off parts of their clothing. But for the older women, respectability demanded that they wore their high collars, long sleeves and voluminous skirts even on the hottest days — it must have been *awful*.

❖ *The men worked in their bare feet and sometimes they'd take
off their shirts you know, but the women, we had to work fully
clothed.*

The machines in the early part of this century were very dangerous indeed. The women in their sixties and fifties did not give any anecdotes of workers having accidents. But almost all of the storytellers in the older group knew of someone who had lost a finger, banged their head or damaged an eye. One woman told of a cousin of hers, a young man of 14, who had lost his life. The youth had somehow become trapped in part of a carding machine and as a result he was crushed. The spinning machines seemed to be have been particularly dangerous, causing some women to lose their fingers.

❖ *A friend of mine, she were wiping her frame end, and all at
once the end of her wiper went through the hole and took her
finger. She lost one finger, right up from her wrist it came right
out, her finger sort of went through the wheels, through the
wheels inside; well, it took her finger clean off.*

According to this storyteller, her employers were not very keen to pay compensation to her friend, despite the fact that they were at fault because the machine on which the woman lost her finger was not properly guarded.

The victim of the accident had to employ the help of a solicitor in order to fight for compensation and apparently the manager of the mill had tried to persuade the former that the accident had occurred as a result of his client's own stupidity. The storyteller explained that she defended her friend. As a result of this defiance the manager was to ensure that she did not move on from spinning to crealing (which was better paid) as long as he remained at that mill. The story is an interesting one. Not only does it bring home the dangerous nature of the mills at this time (this would be about 1930) but it also demonstrates that the workers could be very loyal to each other. The storyteller admitted that she was afraid to contradict the manager because she suspected that he might find a way to punish her for disagreeing with him. She was also very conscious of her own powerless-ness as a worker. Despite these fears she still spoke out for her friend which was a very courageous thing for her to have done. The victim who lost her finger was to receive compensation of £500. But the storyteller told me that this had not been the first accident to have happened on the particular machine. Another friend of her's had lost four fingers and received no compensation at all.

❖ *Mrs X (former worker) — she got four fingers taken off on those new electric frames.*

Another storyteller gave a detailed account of how she had supported a friend trapped in a machine while other workers struggled to free her.

❖ *One of my friends caught her finger in the spinning machine, they had switched it on before she'd had a chance to move it, she'd been cleaning it. Well, I had to hold on to her, I had to stand behind her and hold her while they switched the machines off and got her free. I couldn't bear to look at what was happening to her hands, but I felt all wet on my foot and when I looked down, it was covered in blood . . . she left after that, I don't know if she got any compensation but I do know that she never worked again, her hands were a mess.*

Other storytellers told of accidents which occurred through no apparent fault of the employers — at least not directly. Some told of young women who had suffered injuries because their hair got caught in the straps of the machines because they had failed to keep it tied back. The older workers explained that it was necessary for them to tie their hair back completely in order to avoid accidents. Another storyteller told of a woman who lost an eye when she dropped a spindle which flew back and hit her in the face. This woman's employer had been relatively understanding however and had paid her quite a large amount of compensation for the time (£1000). The storyteller who told this tale remembered that the incident happened just before the Second World War. So it seems that it is not the case that all mill owners were cruel, uncaring people, eager to exploit and mistreat their workers. In addition, it is a measure of social change that attitudes we now consider to be 'cruel' and behaviour which we would now see as deliberate mistreatment used to be thought of as *normal*. When politicians romanticise 'Victorian values' we should remember that for workers, conditions such as those described in this chapter are what such 'values' actually mean. Interestingly, the question of 'Victorian values' was brought up by one storyteller who appeared to have little patience for such rhetoric:

> ❖ *And when you write your book don't forget to mention all those poor children who were strapped to the machines twenty four hours a day will you? That's what the employers did, they got orphans and that and made them work for their keep . . . if you want the history of the mills well that's what its all about, having bits of kids slave away . . . it was before my time that was, but a lot of those I worked with could remember it . . . that's the history of the mills . . . don't forget to mention that will you?*

The slow progress of the introduction of safety measures in the work place, suggests that on the whole, the safety of workers was a very low priority. Workers, it seems, were held responsible for their own safety. Several storytellers gave examples of accidents which happened because of the 'carelessness' of workers. But would we accept such standards today? Would workers in the nineties be prepared to work on a dangerous machine, having simply been told, 'be careful, that's a dangerous machine.' Or would such an alternative, even today, be better for some people than being out of work?

But for all the lack of adequate facilities and the danger, employers could be very good to their workers as well, especially good workers. One woman told of a young unmarried mother who received much generosity from her employers, although her family gave her very little help or sympathy.

> ❖ *There was a young woman who worked there with us, and she got herself into trouble, and of course she had to leave . . . she was only about 18 or 20, or so, and they were good to her, they let her stay on. She could come to work and she didn't need to come till the middle of the morning, when she weren't feeling herself. Then they'd come and let her work till night like, then when she got as she were too big to work, she got her six months leave of absence, then when she got her baby, and she got out of bed after her fortnight, they brought her back to work and took her baby in the nursery and it were only a fortnight old . . . and she worked and they were good to her, but she were a good worker you see.*

Employers it seems, valued good workers. In cases such as the one described above, employers could be more understanding and supportive than the unmarried mother's family. Being an unwed mother may have been socially unacceptable, but it didn't make a bad worker out of a good one. And mills which provided nursery facilities could also help to cater for at least some of the practical problems working mothers faced.

Working conditions in the mills slowly improved as time progressed. Wash-basins were added on the various floors and canteen facilities were provided. The storytellers in their eighties had eaten lunches on their laps, sitting at the end of the frames (machines). Sandwiches, pies and a cup of tea were specked with cotton in an atmosphere of heat, oil and dirt.

The provision of canteen facilities and wash-basins seems to have been the most welcome improvements in the mills. Some workers preferred to go outside, buying a meal from one of the local pie shops or from the chippies. If workers lived nearby they could go home for their dinners. The dinner hour soon passed however. Once workers switched off their machines and walked home there was little time left and eating a meal was a rushed affair as this storyteller remembers.

> ❖ *In that one hour I had for dinner I had to go home, butter the bread, get my dinner ready, have a wash and then go back to work, so it was a rush and really it wasn't a full hour, because the machines were switched off at twelve o'clock, you had to be back at your machine by one o'clock, so you didn't really get an hour you see, I didn't know why they said that you did when we didn't, you see they'd never been fair with us in the mill.*

The canteen in the mill where I worked was very basic. I remember it as a rather small shed located in the far corner of the mill yard. My mother and I did not use it very often because we usually went home for dinner but we did eat there on a few occasions and I remember it as being very clean and the food was well-cooked. But it seemed very basic and overcrowded. It did not seem adequately equipped to accommodate so many workers.

However, I had grown accustomed to the spacious and modern canteen of the local art college. So it could be argued that my perception of the canteen was that of someone who had been, 'spoilt.' Most of the mill workers I interviewed who had eaten regularly in the mill canteen spoke of them in glowing terms. The canteen cooks whose meals I had considered to be so 'basic,' were regarded (by the older mill workers especially) as skilled and talented. The dinner hour was apparently the highlight of the day for some workers. A philosophy of 'waste-not, want-not' proved to be very useful in that it ensured that workers got good value for money. Several workers reported that once the dinners had been served second helpings were made available for all those who wanted them — at no extra cost. The food was of the traditional Northern type, stews, hotpot, various types of pies, puddings of jam roly poly and custard, rice pudding and rhubarb pie, a big favourite in Bolton (see chapter five). It has become the norm in the nineties for people to be careful about their diet. The stodge in meals served to the mill workers would be considered very unhealthy now. We worry about the calories and fat in a jam roly poly, and yet we probably eat more chocolates, crisps and other 'junk foods' than ever before. One of the women interviewed quite unashamedly admitted to having as many as three helpings a time of her canteen cooked jam roly poly and custard. This woman was a healthy eighty-six years of age at the time of her interview. So it may be the case that as long as we burn off the calories (as the women in this study most certainly did) then a bit of stodge and custard might not be as harmful to our health as we are led to believe.

Canteen and toilet facilities were well established by the late sixties. But from the descriptions given during the interviews it would seem that standards between different mills were very diverse. The standard of the washing and toilet facilities provided seems to have depended very much on the goodwill of the employers.

Fine particles of cotton in the atmosphere was another potential health risk which may have increased in later years when huge blowers were introduced to clear the machines of cotton. These blowers were effective in keeping the machines clean but they blew the cotton from the machines into the faces of the workers. Cotton was everywhere. I can remember it itching my nose. If a worker left a drink standing for any length of time a fine film of cotton would develop which floated on the surface.

> ❖ *You had to eat your lunch as you worked in the card room,*
> *but anyway, your food was full of cotton. When the light shone*
> *on it through those big windows, you could see it on your food,*
> *and the same with your brew, so eventually I got a lid off a box*
> *and I took that to work with me and when I brewed up I covered*
> *it then I wouldn't get it full of cotton . . . I've always been*
> *chesty I can't say whether its got anything to do with the cotton*
> *or not, but it can do. I know there was a woman working next*

to me and she was terrible with it and that definitely was the cotton, there is a name for it, I can't remember what its called, but its caused with the cotton, its a disease they get when they work in the mill, and just before I finished there was another woman who started with it. I didn't know that many myself who'd got it, just those two, but I know there was a lot that did get it, but I've got bronchitis quite a lot, but I don't know if it affected me or not. They said the conditions got much better as the years went, but I don't think so, to me it never changed, not to me it didn't.

Byssinosis is a lung disease caused by inhaling cotton which irritates the respiratory system. Byssinosis is a chronic and disabling condition which is quite difficult to differentiate from bronchitis. The woman quoted above admitted to having always suffered from respiratory problems but she is also a smoker. In a case such as hers it may be very difficult to determine to what degree (if any) her bronchial trouble may have been provoked by her exposure to the cotton. Byssinosis (especially in a smoker) may give similar symptoms to bronchitis. So it is very difficult to estimate just how widespread this condition is in Bolton. It would be valid to suggest however, that working in an atmosphere so heavily saturated with fine cotton could be detrimental to the health of the workers.

The cotton got everywhere, as this storyteller remembered, covering the workers' clothes, hair and skin.

❖ *When you were at work you'd think that you'd got all the cotton off you, then you'd come home and you'd look at the carpet behind you and there would be a trail of cotton. You could never wear anything outside that had been worn in the mill because it smelt of stale cotton. You could never have a nice hairdo in the mill, it was all in your hair, your hair was full of this cotton.*

The noise of the machines posed a further threat to the workers' health. In chapter two the noise of the mills was described as one of the most

---

Footnote: thanks to Dr Owen Atkinson, a Bolton GP, for information on Byssinosis

dramatic first impressions encountered by new workers. People did eventually adapt to the noise. But it may well have had some damaging long term effects on people's hearing. Some of the storytellers commented on the frequency of deafness in mill workers. 'Industrial deafness' was often not recognised by doctors (or family and friends). This is because it inhibits normal hearing, especially for normal speech, but does not interfere with (and can actually increase) sensitivity to sounds outside the normal range. The typical story is that of the man who can hear nothing his wife says to him but will hear the neighbours' door close when they go out. This situation could lead to marital strife, especially if the doctor said that there was nothing wrong with the worker's hearing.

❖ *I think it was noisy, weaving is very noisy and nearly all weavers are a bit deaf.*

One of the storyteller's, who suffered from Menière's Disease (this is a hearing problem) felt that her condition had been caused by the noise of the mills.

Despite the dangers, the noise and the cotton, many of the women who took part in the study had fond memories of the mills as well. Many commented during the interviews on the sense of solidarity shared by workers.

❖ *Oh, we used to look after each other in the mills and when I became pregnant with my daughter, they gave me some lovely presents. I made an awful lot of friends in the mills and during the War we used to support each other.*

Younger workers were kept in place under the beady eyes of the older women who were very strict. But the older women were good teachers, not only in the skills of the mill but in those of life as well.

❖ *They were smashing, but the woman we worked with was always shouting. She used to shout, 'come on now, come on.' She used to make us toe the line. She was good, but when her back was turned we were dancing down the alleys, showing each other steps and singing and teaching each other songs. We used to set each others hair in the toilet. There was always someone who could do something like that.*

The task of winding and spinning involved joining, or 'piecing' a strand of cotton from a small bobbin onto a strand from a larger bobbin situated above. Once the two strands had been pieced, the machines wound the cotton from the smaller to the larger bobbin. Each 'side' (a worker's allocated length of machine) had up to 20 ends. Or to put it another way, 20 small bobbins in the process of being wound onto 20 bigger bobbins. Provided the strands of cotton did not break once the worker had pieced them, the ends would be said to be running well. How well a worker's ends ran depended to a large extent on the quality of the cotton. If the quality of the cotton was good then once a worker had pieced up all the ends they could enjoy a short break before the next set of bobbins needed piecing up. These rest periods were put to good use. The women could play cards, go for a smoke and a gossip, or make some extra money crocheting or knitting.

❖ *If you had no doffing for about half an hour (doffers replaced the smaller bobbins in preparation for the spinner piecing this up) we'd go and sit in the toilet, and in't toilets there were a big room and you'd perhaps play cards, or you'd all be talking or singing . . . we were all sort of together because we were about the same age, you were all about sixteen or eighteen and then when you went crealing well that was higher still and the spinners used to come in and they used to teach us how the knit and how to crochet, they'd be making jumpers if their frames were running well. As years went by I learned crocheting and I used to do a lot of mats and I used to crochet gloves as well, and I did knitting, and it came about that some would say, will you knit some for me,' so I used to. I'd charge three and six for a set of mats, half a crown for doing some gloves, and I could do a pair of gloves in a couple of nights and doing a cardigan, I could knit one in a fortnight and a jumper, and I used to charge five*

*shillings for a cardigan or a jumper. We used to buy our wool
from work and our cotton, and it used to be twopence an ounce
for wool and cotton were twopence a ball, four balls made a pair
of mats, two balls made a pair of gloves.*

Men did work in the mills but for the most part appeared to have
been employed in a supervisory role. But the women were far from being
meek and obedient subordinates. A supervisor needed to keep his wits
about him, watching out for younger workers running errands or taking
messages around the mill for the older women — all for the price of a
fag. Apart from the occasional reference to the mule spinners (the men
who had dominated spinning in the past) and the talk of bosses, the
storytellers hardly mentioned men at all. On the basis of this information
it can be assumed that mills were very much a women's world. During
the War years men disappeared from the mills almost completely. Women
took responsibility for the heavier work which had been traditionally
allocated to men.

The storytellers did not appear to feel very positive about women
performing these heavier jobs. They acknowledged that much of the work
that women performed during the Wars, challenged the sexual division
of labour which had existed prior to this. But the jobs the women conducted due to the absence of the men were very unpleasant so that most
considered it a blessing when the latter came back. The only reports of
any serious friction between male and female workers was in connection
with spinning. Mule Spinning was traditionally a male occupation and it
had been better paid and more prestigious than other jobs in the mill.

When modern ring spinning machines were introduced these were
considered suitable for women to work with as well as men. The men
responded by rebelling in various ways. They refused, for example, to let
women spinners join the mule spinners' union. But in general, talk of men
was absent from the stories and conversation centred around women.

When the worker's ends were running well there was time for a break.
It is important to stress that such times were by no means common. If
the cotton failed to run well then work in the mill was very hard. Workers

could be running up and down their frames non-stop all day. This made the work very tiring but it also made the day pass very quickly.

Downstairs in the card room the workers dealt with the cotton in its raw state. The storytellers in this study who had worked in the card room gave the most negative accounts of the mill. There was one exception to this, a woman in her eighties who had worked in the card room all her life and loved it. The stories of the card room overall suggest that this may have been the most unpleasant place of all in which to work.

❖ *Oh, I hated the card room, I used to get my fingers fast and all sorts, I didn't like it at all.*

The data obtained in this study does not provide sufficient evidence to conclude that all card room workers felt negative about their jobs. This discussion may only represent the women who took part in this study. But it is possible that the machinery was noisier and the cotton in its dirty, crude state may have been more unpleasant to work with. Of all the storytellers interviewed it was the card room workers who complained about the mill the most and who spoke of wanting to cry when they had to face work in the mornings. But card room workers like everyone else in the mills took tremendous pride in the work they did. Working in the mill demanded skill.

❖ *I liked weaving, I liked weaving fancy patterns, I enjoyed seeing the colours and studying the pile that they used to put in the cotton. Yes, it was a very skilled job, but I loved pattern weaving, I loved it.*

By the late sixties young people in Bolton had greater opportunities open to them. Fewer people leaving school were going into the mill and for some reason mill girls were beginning to get a reputation of being 'common.' The storytellers in their fifties and sixties were aware of this and commented on it. But this was not the case for the older women. So this rather negative stereotype seems to have been a late development in the history of the mills and may have been an indication of their coming demise (see the discussion in chapter eight). I was influenced by the stereotype myself. This was despite the fact that I came from a family of women who worked in the mill and who were far from 'common.' Stereotypes are very powerful so that we all tend to be influenced by them, unless we have experiences which challenge them. When I went to work in the mill I found that women who worked there were certainly not 'common'.

The young and older women I worked with had what would be considered high moral standards (especially in the nineties) and this seems to have been a strong characteristic of mill workers. I found the mill to be a storehouse of wasted talent. The workers were often gifted in some way but had missed opportunities. Yet this was at a time when greater opportunities (in theory) were opening up to working class people. I was surprised to find just how skilled the job of winding which I was employed to do was. I learned that working with cotton was not a job for the ignorant or unskilled. Workers had to develop a feel for the cotton, a feel which came about with experience. When you have worked with cotton for a time you learn to distinguish between good and bad yarn.

Workers had to learn to appreciate the right feel to their cones (large bobbins) in order to know if they had done their job properly. They had to understand their machines and recognise the way the thread was running in order to be able to spot if something was wrong. This knowledge of cotton possessed by the women of the mills was of an intuitive, experiential nature which is difficult to describe. Understanding cotton is a state of being. It can only be understood by those who have experienced it. Once you become sensitive to the feel of fabric, then this becomes as important (if not more important) then the look of a garment at least 'on the peg.' A fabric of good quality always hangs beautifully on the wearer anyway. Most of the women I interviewed were aware of the fact that they had this intuitive knowledge of cotton and they took great pride in it. This skill made the mill workers of Bolton very shrewd shoppers. It was once very common in Bolton to see women rubbing the fabric of a garment between their fingers when deciding whether or not to buy — you don't see people doing that now. My mother had this feel for cloth. She was, and still is, a connoisseur of fabrics.

Some owners of the mills were very progressive providing a good, clean working environment for their workers and in addition sports and recreation facilities, a practice going back to the 19th century (see Robert Poole's 'Popular Leisure and the Music Hall in 19th-century Bolton'). Eagley Mill provided a bowling green for the workers as early as 1840. One storyteller in her early sixties at the time of interview told of a mill where she had worked during the early fifties. The owners of this mill had created a lovely park, tennis courts, a sports club and a dance hall which was used by the workers at the weekends. The storyteller assured me that the cost to workers in order to enjoy all these facilities was very low. When asked how they felt about the decline of the textile industry in Bolton, the storytellers were very ambivalent. On the one hand, they felt saddened that such a large part of Bolton life and heritage was disappearing. They also regretted that a source of employment for Bolton people had been lost. Many of the women who took part in this study would have preferred not to have gone in to the mills. But at least it was a job. Despite these regrets the storytellers were thankful that future generations would not have to face the unpleasant working conditions, the heat and the long hours of the mills. But for all their unpleasantness the mills should be remembered. Thousands of our forebears worked in them and their labour helped to make Bolton the town that it is today. We owe it to our forebears to remember the mills, to preserve their history as a tribute to them. But for the benefit of anyone tempted to romanticise the cotton mills, it would be useful to remember the words of one of the storytellers interviewed.

❖ *People of my generation will tell you exactly what I've told you: they wouldn't go back in the mills for a thousand pounds a day.*

CHAPTER FOUR

ROMANCE AND MARRIAGE

I've got a boyfriend. We can't get married just yet because he has to grow up and get a job. My family don't know about him (well Marilyn does; she's got one, too) and if they do find out about him they're sure to disapprove — I hope. I know from the telly, love's only fun if your family disapprove because then your boyfriend can rescue you.

I've left home a couple of times because I want to be grown up and have my own house, but I can't afford a telly just yet so I keep having to come back to watch 'Ivanhoe'. My teacher sent a letter home, 'Christine cannot spell 'Cat' but she can spell 'Ivanhoe'. You see why I want to be grown up? I'm sick of having to put up with the childishness of adults. I've got a few ideas. I could build a tree house or live in a tent. Anyway, I've decided all that's too hard, so I'm going to wait until my boyfriend grows up, then he can buy me a house with electricity and I can carry on watching 'Ivanhoe' and 'Lost in Space'. The disadvantage of all this is that I have to put up with him and even worse, court with him until he's old enough to be a proper man.

Courting is pretty boring. We do all our courting in a big black box in the yard and we have to take turns with Marilyn and her boyfriend. We learnt about courting from the telly. What you do is, you stare into each others eyes — this means you're in love. It shows it on the telly all the time, the camera flashes from his eyes to her eyes, his eyes, her eyes and so on . . . so we usually spend about five or ten minutes with our boyfriends (me and Marilyn) staring at each other. As a matter of fact our boyfriends look really daft when they look at us like that. I wonder if they think the same about us? I suppose they must since we're trying just as hard. As a matter of fact, I don't like courting, it's pretty boring. To be honest I'd finish with him except that if I do he might *not* break his heart, which would make me look a right fool. So I suppose I'll just have to put up with it.

This is another of those nonsituated memories, did all this happen before or after we were in Cyprus? My Dad was in the Armed Forces and we went to Cyprus for three years. Now this black box is in some way connected, but I can't remember how — is this before or after Cyprus? No matter, the box was useful anyhow. It was symbolic for my sister and me of a period of maturation — we knew by this time that adults did more than go shopping together — they stared at each other as well.

As a young child I can remember knowing that adult relationships, especially between married couples, were in some way special. But I could never put my finger on what was special about them — I'd tried the staring and frankly, I hadn't found that special at all. I had recognised that there were other important themes connected with these relationships, such as touch, intense feeling and (sometimes) a sort of comfortable closeness. I also understood that love, marriage and a house came together, and in that order.

There is a myth about the society of my youth, the late fifties and early sixties. The myth is that children were at this time unaware of sex* — and yet, if they were, how is it that I remember so clearly being aware of something? Of course, we didn't have the explicit knowledge that quite young children have today. Sexual* matters are discussed much more openly in the nineties: sex education and the media have all helped to take care of that. So the majority of children understand that courting couples do a lot more than stare (who knows? — they might not bother even doing that). Children generally have a good sexual vocabulary too, but are they necessarily more aware of sexuality in its fullest sense than we were at this age? They still seem to develop the same myth of the invisibility of sexuality which led us to project an image of asexuality onto older people. Perhaps young people always believe that sex is today's discovery — our

---

* *See footnote at end of chapter*

Mum and Dad didn't do it did they? The myth promotes a naive belief which persists beyond childhood telling us that older people have always been reluctant about sex — if they did it at all it was probably a mistake, and they certainly won't talk about it.

> ❖ *He got hold of my hand, and he said, 'I love you, I love you,' and he was stroking my hand like this, oh it was lovely, he pulled me over, oh, and he gave me the most lovely kiss. It was lovely, the most passionate of all kisses ... and I knew then that he loved me, just like he'd done when we'd started out as a courting couple, I knew he loved me just the same ... Oh, I often think of that kiss, I think of him constantly you know Christine, and within an hour of giving me that kiss he was dead.*

Youth. What does this word mean? We associate the concept of youth with chronological age, but the storyteller quoted above was 86 years old when she told me this story. As she recalled that kiss, an affirmation of their first youthful, romantic, loving encounter, her whole being, skin, eyes, aura, took on the glow and optimism of a young woman deeply in love.

This story gives just one example of a strong theme which emerged from the older women's discussions of their relationships — the narrative of touch. The narrative of touch surprised me at first because I began my interviews with the naive belief that older people do not discuss their sexuality. It came as a surprise to find that older women do discuss sexuality* quite openly. It was true that their stories were not as explicit as younger people's but in my view, the indirect nature of their love talk made it all the more beautiful. A writer called Roland Barthes has put forward the view that romance has become the present day taboo. Whereas in the past, sexual language was obscene, romance was acceptable and widely discussed. The situation has now been reversed. My storytellers, whose values were formed before the present day, helped to confirm this view: they had some inhibitions in expressing their sexual experiences using a romantic vocabulary of sentimentality and sensuality, but they avoided any explicit sexual language.

❖ *We were a very fortunate couple, we were very happy and we used to do things for each other. When I was tired he used to rub my feet with oil, and put some cream on, oh it was lovely, it was nice.*

The practice of stroking and rubbing parts of a loved ones body is a theme which frequently came up in the conversations I had with the older women but unfortunately not all of the anecdotes were picked up on the tape. The older women seemed more at ease talking of their intimate relationships once the tape was switched off, so that I am left with very few examples of what was actually said. Perhaps there had been something in my belief that older people will not discuss intimate matters after all. I feel, however, that the narrative of touch should be mentioned in this book because it challenges the idea that older people do not and may never have experienced, sexual feelings. Our society strips older people of their sexuality (especially the disabled elderly). Then we behave as if there was no sexuality to strip away in the first place. It is hard for us to imagine that older people have sexual feelings, that they once loved and made love. In many respects, the narrative of touch suggests that the older generation are more aware of a dimension of sexuality which can be greatly neglected today — that of touch. Touching is among the most sensual sexual experiences. Our present day preoccupation with orgasm could lead us to forget the pleasures of touch, of being stroked or rubbed with oil, all the pleasures shared by these older women and their husbands.

For the most part, intimacy was an experience people only shared if they were married. The women all commented on (especially those in their eighties) the ways in which attitudes towards sexuality have changed, and few approved. The women had very traditional views about gender and the 'proper' behaviour of young women.

❖ *Well, its not like it is now. Me mam used to say, 'there's no decent young woman parades herself around the streets after the pubs are closed.' Yes, she did, and that's why we weren't allowed out during the week, because she used to say, 'I'm not having you parading around the streets after dark, asking for trouble.'*

The women in their eighties at the time of the interviews reported that they had been regulated and controlled by their parents until they were well into their twenties. This was the case even if they were involved in a long standing relationship.

❖ *Every Saturday night we used to go out. Me mother wouldn't let us go out through the week, we always had to be in for ten o' clock on a Saturday ... and I were going with my husband, I were bringing him in and we had to run down Blackburn Road from the theatre to be in for ten o' clock (both laugh). Yes, and I were courting steady then, he were coming in the house.*

The storytellers of the older age group also told of being severely punished if they broke the rules society imposed on 'nice young women.'

❖ *I were 26 years old and I were coming up Blackburn Road, we'd been to the pictures with some lads, and she were coming up the street and I thought 'oh, god, me mother,' and we ran up the street, then she wouldn't see us ... but she had and, oh, didn't she slap my face.*

Despite the strict upbringing experienced by the older women, no one gave any indication of any feelings of resentment towards their parents. Many of the anecdotes, such as the one given above, were given with a hint of affection. The older women however, seemed to have adopted 'correct' feminine behaviour of their own free will, because they believed such conduct to be right and proper. Others reported that the long hours in the mill made them feel too tired for late nights and boyfriends anyway.

❖ *I used to come home tired. Sometimes I'd come home so tired I couldn't eat my tea, I'd just want a cup of tea, I'd not want any tea, I was really, really tired.*

When couples did go out together They spent their time in the temperance bars, the theatres and church meetings. The young courting couple were often with a group of young people rather than spending time alone. But despite the outward display of respectability, young couples did find time to show each other affection, even though this was closely surveyed by the watchful eyes of parents.

Chris — Did you ever get any time alone together, you and your husband when you were courting?

❖ *Oh, yes, we stood in the vestibule, we'd chat and have a cuddle there, that's how we got a chance to be alone . . . our parents didn't mind that . . . they'd shout every now and again, 'come on now, its getting late,' and all that (laughs). They were keeping an eye on you like, but oh, we had a kiss and a cuddle in't vestibule.*

I wonder what effect this close proximity of parents had on the young couple enjoying a quiet cuddle in the tiny, semi public space of the vestibule. Did it frustrate the couple, or simply add to the excitement? We all know the saying, 'it's naughty, but it's nice.' Did the expression of sexuality under such circumstances make the experience perhaps even naughtier, even nicer, even though it must have been restricted to touch? This storyteller's account (quoted above) given I might add, with nostalgic delight, suggests that kissing in a vestibule, ever conscious of the watchful eyes and ears of parents, might well have been a very stimulating experience precisely because it needed to be controlled. Sometimes, public places as well, had their allocated spot for the courting couple, such as at the back of the local theatre.

❖ *If you were courting and you liked a bit of kissing, well, you went downstairs.*

In addition to providing private space for lovers, the theatres, I was told, put on some pretty good shows. Courtship was lengthy and a young couple could be walking out together a year or more before they committed themselves to that first kiss.

❖ *We went together for twelve months before we even kissed
each other and then when we did get married it was beautiful,
it always was.*

Although some of the older women did discuss sex, it was always in
this rather veiled narrative in which the act of sex was never mentioned
directly. Some of the women commented on the lack of sexual knowledge
in their youth and considered this to be a bad thing. They felt however
that the pendulum now had swung a little too much in the opposite
direction.

❖ *I mean, it's the same with sex, it was bad when they didn't
know anything at all. My husband had seven sisters and he
didn't even know till he married about periods, and there were
some who didn't even know where kids came from . . . but now,
oh its gone too far, its all sex, sex, sex . . .*

Chris — *What you seem to be saying about your relationship
with your husband is that there was more romance and less
emphasis on sex.*

❖ — *Yes, and I think it was better, I think sex is a very private thing
between a man and his wife, I don't think it should be talked about, I
think its private, I never discussed my sex life with my husband with
anyone else, I don't think he did, sex is everywhere now.*

Entry into the young woman's home, was it seems, a very significant
step in the relationship, indicating that the relationship was becoming
more serious.

❖ *When we got older and we were noticing the lads me mam
said, 'now if you start going with lads like,' she said, 'I don't
want any messing.' She said 'I don't want any lads coming in
this house until you're ready to go out with them, so make your
mind up whether you want them or not, I'm not having any
Tom, Dick or Harry coming in this house.'*

The lengthy business of courtship usually began with the young woman playing hard to get with a bashful young man. Then the women in their seventies and eighties discussed their husbands prior to the beginning of the courtship, as a shadow following them around. The women seemed to take tremendous pride in the knowledge that they had been admired from afar. In response to this admiration they reported a cool indifference.

❖ *When I was 19, I'll always remember, he used to be my shadow, he was always hanging around. I used to have a bike and he used to say, 'can I pump your tyre up.' From being 14 he was always there.*

The apparent shyness of some young men led them to asking a woman out via a friend. This arrangement was useful for both parties. It saved the young man's face in the event of a refusal and it also gave the woman an opportunity to check out the former's character before she committed herself.

❖ *Mary said, 'Jack wants to know if you'll go out with him', and I said, 'Well, I don't know, I don't know if I like him or not,' I said 'He seems a bit quiet, what's he like?' and she said, 'oh, go on, you'll like him, he's nice and he likes you, he's a nice lad and he doesn't swear.'*

All the women in this study report solid, conventional 'upright,' lives, especially with regard to sexual and courtship matters. But the storytellers of all age groups told tales of the 'Jezebel.' Most mills had at least one young woman who defied authority, especially with regard to sexual conventions. Such women were the butt of many a sarcastic remark but nonetheless were afforded much attention, almost envy by the other mill girls when it came to the tea breaks.

❖ *One used to come with some right spanking stories, everyone was quite content to listen to her, quite a character she was, she liked to change her boyfriends quite a lot, and she was very open, and she told us everything and it made Lady Chatterley's Lover look like Enid Blyton, so it was very interesting listening to*

Karen's sagas. We never showed too much shock because we were frightened of her not telling us things, so we all looked as if what she was saying was all normal and natural, but actually inside we were collapsing with shock (both laugh).

From what the storytellers seemed to be saying, the unconventional women were admired by the ordinary mill girls, who (despite their improper courtship manners) seemed to wish they had the courage to do the same things themselves. One of the older storytellers knew a young woman who shocked everyone, not only the other women because of her refusal to be 'proper' but in her total disregard for the rules of the mills as well. This latter affront to convention appeared to cause great delight to the women working with her.

❖ — *Oh, and when the Yanks come, a girl who worked with me, she used to go home on a Friday, and many a time she didn't come back tilt' following Wednesday. She'd be with the Yanks, she wouldn't come back to work and she'd get a good cussing, but she didn't bother (laughs) as she were having a good time with the Yanks.*

But the women in their seventies and eighties demanded impeccable behaviour (and character) from a potential suitor. Drinking and swearing were definitely out, the young man had to be respectful of older people and working. When I listened to the stories of early courtship and marriage given by these older women, I was surprised to realise how very different the ideal man of their time was from the hard drinking, macho image of manhood promoted by the media today. The ideal man for these women seemed to be gentle, shy, teetotal and hard working. The symbol of a good husband was one who handed over his wage packet, unopened, to his wife. Just how many married men lived up to this ideal it is difficult to say, but the women in this study where quite clear about the fact that this was what they expected of a husband, and this is what they got. One woman did comment (with deep disapproval) on a friend whose husband failed to hand over the unopened wage packet.

❖ — *Now her husband liked a bet on't horses. Every now and*
again he'd win, not so often, but when he did, oh, she'd be in her
element, because he'd treat her to a new coat, or something daft and
she'd say, 'oh look he's bought me such and such,' and I used to
think, 'well how can he be treating you if he's only giving you
what he should be giving you anyway? Why, you can buy your
own coat, with your own money if he'd give you what he should'.

The woman explained that the unopened wage packet was necessary
when they married because wages were so low that there was no room
for individual family members to keep back money for themselves. However, all the women reported giving their husbands pocket money, although the amount varied according to how much could be afforded each
week — the women did not, it seems, give themselves pocket money. I
do not know how general this practice of handing over wage packets was
at this time in history, but I do know that it was a very important symbol
of a good marriage in Bolton for many years (I can remember my father
handing over his wage packet to my mother). There may have been many
incentives for men and women to encourage this practice, in addition to
the greater economic power the mills made possible for women of the
time. The churches may have played their part in encouraging it, but in
addition there was the fact that the men could be at any time, unemployed
while their wives were in work. So the promotion of a little give and take
was sensible. Many of the older women in the study reported having to
maintain their husbands at some time — and they still gave them spending
money whenever possible. It might not have served the best interests of
the men of Bolton (at least in the long term) to foster selfishness in a
marriage. It is by no means the case, however, that all husbands handed
over their wage packets unopened, although those who did not were
greatly frowned on because of the hardship this caused their wives and
families.

❖ — *Well, the wage was too small to be splitting up you see.*
A man's wage, especially if the wife wasn't working, had to
cover everything, the rent, the food and everything, so if a man

started taking out of his wage, it caused hardship on the family, and a man that did that was frowned on by men and women alike, and they always put their families in a bad spot. I lived in an area which was nearly all mill workers, and round that area at least, I could count on one hand the men who kept their wages and left their families short, but the men who did it were frowned upon, really as a lower moral class of man. The women who was married to that kind of man needed an awful lot of help, but the men who were mean with their wives I could count on one hand, and the women just had to put up with it, I mean where could they go, because most people were living in very small accommodation, so even their parents couldn't take in a ready made family, and wages weren't that good if you was a working woman.

So it was important to check out a potential suitor. If you made a 'poor choice,' and selected as a husband someone who would not provide, then as a woman, you were trapped. There was no escape from an unhappy marriage in the time of these storytellers' youth. Women were very much at the mercy of the goodwill of husbands, and although it is clear that there was much social pressure put on men to be 'good providers,' not all men were responsive to this. At the risk of romanticising marriages of the past however, it seems that at least for the women who took part in this study that marriage was a very loving experience.

My experience of the men in my own family (and in the neighbourhood) was that, despite the external image of toughness which tended to be promoted, in the private domain of the family they were gentle and sensitive. One memory which springs to mind is of an afternoon I spent with my maternal grandfather, Joseph Steptoe. I would be about nine at the time and he would be about seventy. We walked slowly up the gradual slope of Church Road in Bolton, stopping every now and then, while he caught his breath. I was used to his deep, steady respirations by now and considered them a familiar and comforting sound, a reminder that he was there.

Sitting on the park, we met up with some of my friends. Grandad had fallen asleep and his breath was more laboured, as it always was when he slept.

A friend of mine came over to talk and expressed concern about Grandad's breathing, she assured me that it wasn't normal.

Walking back, I asked Grandad why was it that his breathing was so 'funny'. He laughed, grasped my tiny shoulder in his enormous hand and reminded me that he was getting older. I felt reassured by this, but started paying more attention to his breathing. My friend was right, there was something funny about it and it was getting worse.

Gradually it became harder and harder for him to exert himself. The bed was brought downstairs and he lay in it most of the time, facing the telly. Occasionally I would pop on the bed and lie at the side of him to watch the 'Beverley Hill-Billies'.

'We like this, don't we, love?' he would say.

'Yes, Grandad,' I would answer.

I noticed that the mattress was rippling underneath me because of the sheer physical effort it was taking him to breathe. The rippling effect felt soothing and cosy. I did not think about it beyond that.

When they brought the coffin in, Grandmother asked me if I wanted to say goodbye. I said that I did, so she took my hand and guided me to the coffin. His chest was odd, deflated. What was wrong? 'They took his lungs for research' the undertaker said. His eyes, once so full of life, had lost their sparkle — they stared, wide open, fixed at the ceiling. I found my attention focusing on his huge hands, the hands of a worker — they would never hold me again.

Grandma was in the kitchen when she realised he was going.

'How did you know?' I asked.

'Because the birds stopped singing,' she replied.

Footnotes: in this chapter:–

'Sex' is used as a general term

'Sexual matters' refers to the technicalities of sex.

'Sexuality' refers to experience of sexual matters.

CHAPTER FIVE

WORKING-CLASS MUMS

All this happened a long time ago. These memories of mothers and fathers, my own parents and other people's are very fragmented.

I love this, all the women are coming into my mother's house. I've got to get under the table quick, then I can listen in. Women's chatter — I loved it when I was small. Hidden under the table I could listen to all the latest gossip, who'd got married, who'd been to the baby shop in town for a new brother or sister. In my childhood mind, I had conjured up an image of a big discount store in town where people bought babies. This was my way of explaining to myself the sudden appearance of my brother and sister. I reckoned they'd not got such a bargain when they bought them — Marilyn and Leonard. Marilyn was always crying and Leonard hardly spoke at all.

It's dark and musty under here. As they talk I make myself comfortable, positioning myself between two clawed feet of the table. I can feel a screw from the centre of the table rubbing on my scalp. I got my hair caught in one of those once. Women's feet — fascinating things. Small and dainty, cased in open sandals. Painted toe nails — I wonder why? Everyone knows it's just not true. People don't have red toe nails. How silly to think they can fool anyone. Grown-ups — you'll never fathom them out.

Other feet are encased in tombs of leather or patent, thick wads of flesh puffing up from the cutting edge of the shoe. Some of the older women wear thick stockings which gives the skin an odd surface sheen like sausage skins. Some women wear no stockings at all. Floury white flesh sprout from the cotton frock, speckled here and there with thread veins, blue and red.

Stump! The teapot is placed back on the table. A familiar scratching sound indicates that butter is being scraped on home made scones; I'll sneak downstairs tonight to pinch some of those. It'll be a while before they start talking proper. I'll just draw on my doll for a bit — if I can find a space. Oh . . . they've started!

I am supposed to be hidden in this reconstructed memory. Nevertheless, I can recall the image of a hand pulling the table cloth to one side and a female face checking on me. There are some annoying parts of the conversation where they all talk in whispers. Somewhere in the background I can hear my brother and sister talking, well, Marilyn talking to I *assume*, Leonard. That kid! It doesn't matter if she's crying or chattering. There's always some kind of noise coming out of her.

I got earache a lot when I was a child (at least, that's what I remember). I'm in the vestibule making a lot of noise. I want my mother to come and sit down then I can push myself into her, then the pain will go away. Here she is. She puts her arm around me and I push my face as hard as possible into her. There — it's gone.

It's evening in our house. This memory's very misty. I can just make out in the fog a coal fire, a man slumped in a chair and a tin bath in the corner of the room. I'm warm, so I must have just been in there. There's no Mum in the house. I suppose this memory's about the time when she worked evenings. Marilyn is talking to my brother Leonard — as usual. Actually, I'm getting used to having a brother and sister around, they are sort of cute. We'll be going to bed soon and I'll have to tell Marilyn a story — I've not decided what it's going to be on yet, I think I'll make it about the moon. Marilyn's got a thing about moons and fish — funny isn't it, she married a fish in later life, David Fish.

My mother had always worked. I can't remember there ever being a time when she didn't have a job. Later on in life when I heard the academic debates on the topic of working mothers I wondered what all the fuss was about. Mums did work. They always had. And when the pro-housewife lobby talked of the deprivation suffered by children whose mothers did work, I felt even more confused. I certainly didn't feel deprived in any way.

Bolton has a long history of working mothers, especially in the textile industry. Yet family life was still, at least in principle, very traditional. Husbands were the heads of households — and it was considered a father's responsibility to maintain his family financially. However, the low wages of many husbands meant that a wife's financial contribution to the household was far more than pin money. There were times my storytellers assured me, when a woman's wage had to maintain the whole family, due to long periods during which their husbands were unemployed.

> ❖ *I lived for two years and five months without a penny off my husband, and I kept us all that time, and he used to do all the housework while I was at work. We had to keep our jobs because there was a lot of dole then and you never knew if your husband would be in a job or not, and my husband were out of work all that time and once he'd drawn his money out, that were it, I never got a penny off him . . . so if you had a job you had to stick to it, you couldn't just give it up because you'd got married.*

There were examples in the textile industry of women who could earn more than men.

> ❖ *Our women would be better earners than the men, because a lot of them had hands like shovels dealing with very fine yarn. Well, women are nimble piecing up and everything, they could be earning more than the men.*

There were also a lot of women who were coping with bringing up children alone for various reasons, death of a spouse, abandoned women, the War years caused lone parenthood for many families which could be temporary or permanent. In many households, reunited couples experienced terrible marital problems after the War which sometimes led to family breakdown. The division of labour therefore in Bolton households varied considerably, despite the romantic ideal of a family headed by a male breadwinner. Regardless of whether women worked or not however, the home was a woman's domain. This was a place where women gathered to share child minding responsibilities, shopping and cooking tips, at least during the days. In the evenings, at least in those families which had managed to stay together despite the various traumas life inflicted on ordinary people, a lot of men stayed at home with their families. Of the 14 women I interviewed, all reported that they had husbands who stayed out of the pub during the week. The pub it seems, was once a place in which largely older people socialised. Men who did spend too much time in the pub were greatly frowned upon — and I think 'too much' meant more then a couple of nights a week.

> ❖ *The entertainments changed. They go to pubs and clubs now, more pubs than we did in our time, like when we were teenagers especially, we never thought of going into a pub, we never thought of doing it when we were married. They had temperance bars, it was like a shop where they sold groceries and all that, and you could go in and there was like tables in. We'd have a pop and a cup of tea, but there was a lot of bad feeling about drink then you know, there was a lot of temperance meetings then against drink, but such that most of us were brought so strict you'd never dream of going into a pub, nobody thinks anything about it now do they, and then there wasn't the money knocking about then that there is today.*

It was pointed out during the interviews that some people must have frequented the pubs, otherwise the businesses would have collapsed. The storytellers acknowledged this but still insisted that going in the pub was disapproved of and because younger people were strictly brought up they tended to avoid parental chastisement. Therefore, people tended to be much older when they started going into pubs than they tend to be today.

> ❖ *— Oh, yes, but it was frowned on, very much frowned on, you were brought up so strict you'd never dream of going in a pub, it was mostly older people used to do it. It was a bit of a funny thing for a woman, she wouldn't go into a pub on her own, she*

might go in if she had a friend. Older women used to go in and have a drink, it was something older people did really, there was a lot of it amongst older people, whereas now it's reversed, it's all younger people now, but then you'd feel out of place, a young person in a pub, it was a place for old people.

My mother worked in the evenings, employing a local girl to look after my sister and brother and myself until my father got home. But how did mothers cope who worked full time? During the course of the interviews, many of the storytellers told of local mills which provided the workers with nurseries for their children. These nurseries were particularly useful when both husband and wife worked in the same mill, especially after the introduction of shift work. Some employers were prepared to arrange matters so that the couple could work opposite shifts.

❖ *I knew of one couple who had a baby and they worked on opposite shifts, and so what they did was, say one was coming on at two o' clock, one would bring the baby with them and leave it in the nursery those few minutes till the other who was finishing would pick the baby up and take it home, and that's how they got by and I can remember them telling me about having to leave notes for each other because they saw so little of each other, working full time.*

It came as a surprise to learn that some of the mills had to close their nurseries down because of a lack of demand from the workers. Apparently, women generally preferred to make their own private child minding arrangements, depending on friends or other family members, in particular the grandmother. The nurseries provided by the employers were convenient and from the accounts given, provided an excellent standard of child care. But the fees could leave a sizeable hole in a worker's wage packet. Friends and relatives were cheaper. But as the size of a family grew, work outside the home became more difficult. Grandmothers often found the strain of looking after two or more young children too great. Looking after a few children in a tiny two up two down cottage must have added to the strain, so that sooner or later, mothers would have to take a temporary break from full-time work.

❖ *I finished work for a few years after my third baby. They were very sorry to see me go, but I said to the boss, 'well, I can't expect my Mother to look after three young 'uns.' They were all very small you see, so then I had to leave, and it wasn't until my youngest started school that I went back.*

Given the poverty of the older women's time, an extra wage must have been considered very necessary. Life must have been extremely difficult when the family became too large for grandmothers to cope with child minding. Some women, such as my Mother, overcame the problem by working in the evening but such employment was not always available. Limiting family size was unthinkable to the older group and there was little (if any) information available on contraception anyway.

Chris: — *Was there any information about contraception then?*

❖ *No, not like there is now, there was nothing like that. Nobody had heard of anything like that then, no one even thought of it you know, you just got married and the children came, or, the children didn't come, it was like that . . . unless some had heard, you know, those who didn't want children, but mostly people just had them.*

Some people clearly did know about contraception however, because one of the storytellers admitted that she and her husband limited their family. This storyteller had experienced a long and difficult labour when she delivered her only child, a daughter. The couple had decided that ,'she wasn't going through that again,' so there were no more children. This storyteller did not go on to discuss how she and her husband avoided a further pregnancy and it seemed inappropriate to probe for further information during the interview. The storyteller had already given some quite intimate information and to seek more than she offered seemed rather an intrusion. Contraceptive information does seem to have been hard to obtain in the older women's youth, and this may not have been helped by the attitude of the medical profession. It would seem from what some of the older women reported that some doctors at that time did not approve of people using contraception and they could be very judgemental of women who were suspected of taking steps to limit their families.

One older woman (aged 86 at the time of interview) told of an incident she experienced when, at the age of twenty three she started bleeding vaginally. When the woman sought medical help she was cross examined by a very unpleasant doctor who was apparently, very rude to her indeed, until he found out for sure that she had not been trying to induce an abortion. He later apologised for believing the storyteller to be 'a woman like that' (one who gets rid of her baby). The woman, in fact, was not pregnant at all.

My maternal grandmother told me about 'French Letters' when I married. She had apparently encountered them for the very first time when she saw some washed ashore on Blackpool beach. She thought condoms had earned their nickname because they had originated in France. According to many of the storytellers, knowledge of condoms infiltrated the working class public after the Second World War.

Some of the younger women told of a new method of contraception which became available in the fifties, the reusable condom. Disposable condoms were available in the fifties but the thicker, economy condom could be washed and used again and again (kind to the environment as well). However, the reusable condom was to prove rather expensive for one of the storytellers because whenever the couple had an argument it was thrown to the back of the open fire because, 'we won't be needing this again.' It is clear from the storytellers' accounts that contraceptive information was widely available to the general public by the fifties, although methods were restricted to the condom (reusable for the thrifty) the rhythm method, coitus interruptus and for some couples, complete abstinence.

But despite the limited range of contraceptive methods which were available at this time, the new awareness evident in the fifties suggests that people were becoming knowledgeable about thier bodies, their sexuality, and of the reproductive process in general. In a very short time, forty or so years, there has been a rapid change in social attitudes towards sexuality, which may have been accelerated by the War years.

Menstruation was another area in which peoples knowledge had improved and in which the provision of sanitary protection had become commercialised. The older women reported that when they were younger, menstruation was not talked about. Many girls found out about their monthly cycle once it started and not before. One older woman reported that her husband did not find out about menstruation until he married, despite the fact that he had six sisters. If it is the case that menstruation was hushed up then it must have been very difficult for women to be discreet when they menstruated in such small, overcrowded houses. The older women had not used disposable sanitary protection, home made towels were used. These towels came in the shape of fabric squares. Two of the corners were hooped and the towel was held in place with a sanitary belt. The storytellers insisted that the towels provided very good, comfortable protection and they were easy to clean. Women soaked the towels in buckets of cold water under the sink, then washed them and hung them out to dry in the back streets. The men, it appeared, never seemed to be curious about what they were. The availability of sanitary protection was also influenced by social class. One older storyteller in her eighties told of starting her period whilst visiting her future husband's family. Her fiancé's family were relatively middle class and one of the sisters gave the storyteller a disposable towel. This was the first time the storyteller had ever seen such a thing. She insisted however, that the disposable towel was not as comfortable as her home made protection. It might be expected that the home made towels could be uncomfortable and unhygienic. But some of the storytellers challenged this point of view when it was put forward at interview arguing that much of the disposable protection used in the nineties is far from healthy, especially tampons.

❖ *Well, it's not so hygienic today is it? You hear all about these tampons, they've killed a few people them and these sanitary towels that they have now, well they block up toilets and all sorts. It wasn't so bad, they could rub like, but apart from that they were alright and you didn't mind washing them, it was no trouble, you just got used to it, I mean those tampons, I don't think its natural. It should come away, I think. I knew women who had to use old rags, old shirts and all sorts, there were some who didn't wear anything at all way back you know, God knows how they went on. So you were well off, things were looking up when you had these towels. You made them yourself, got some towelling, or sometimes old nappies, and cut out these squares and hemmed them, you'd make so many and then store them in your drawers like, till you needed them. They were a jolly good idea, I'll tell you.*

If it is the case that some women once wore nothing at all, their flow being absorbed as this older storyteller remembered, by their long skirts, then home made towels must have been a welcome improvement. The discomfort and soreness caused by a lack of adequate sanitary protection must have been unbearable for these women, especially when working in the heat of the mills.

The older women in the study had given birth to their children in their own homes. It was towards the latter end of the War, according to the storytellers when women started going into hospital to have their children. Childbirth was considered to be a delicate episode in a woman's life in the early part of this century. After the delivery the mother had to stay in bed for two weeks. This was called the 'lying in' period.

The storytellers seemed to have mixed feelings about the 'lying in' period. On the one hand it was felt that this confinement to bed was unnecessary and it could be very boring for the mother. But some of the women in the study also pointed out that the lying in period did ensure that mothers got a proper rest after the delivery We are frequently told in the nineties that pregnancy and giving birth are not an illness. While this is true, labour can be hard work and very exhausting. As the story-teller quoted below points out, husbands in the nineties can all too often leave the bulk of household responsibilities to their wives very soon after

they have given birth. The 'lying in' period however, may have encouraged some husbands to take on at least some household responsibilities
after the delivery, so that their wives could have a few days' rest.

❖ *I had both of my babies at home, I didn't go into hospital,*
I had them both at home because they had midwives in them
days, that used to come and of course if you needed a doctor,
which I did both times, they used to come, but it's funny they
didn't rush you in them days. I mean, they are out in two days
now, aren't they, Then they are rushing about doing all their
housework, they don't get a proper rest at all, whereas in them
days you stayed in bed a fortnight . . . well, my husband used to
help, and my mother used to come round. My husband worked
nights but he still had to help, because you were in bed you see,
now they are expected to be up and get on with it. You could
get up for little bits of things then but the idea was that you
were supposed to rest, whereas now you are up and out. It's all
changed now, in some respects it's easier, but in some instances,
especially for women now, its a lot harder. I know of quite a lot
who have had to go back for haemorrhages and that, infections,
there seems to be a lot of that now.

Middle-class women were expected to stay in bed for a month so that
social class was an additional influence on woman's experience of childbirth. Home deliveries seem to have been a family affair, at least for older
members of the family so that it may have been less common in the early
part of this century for mothers to feel socially isolated. One older woman
gave a detailed account of her home delivery and of the involvement of
people outside the family. This woman's story is a remarkable account of
how people in her youth would go to great lengths to help others, even
complete strangers. This storyteller experienced a long and difficult labour.
The doctor in attendance had sent the woman's sister for another doctor's
help. The second doctor, having been summoned by the sister, came out
of his surgery, stopped a passing car and asked the driver to take him
to the woman's house, which the driver did. The driver then waited in

his car outside the house until he was assured by the doctors that his services were no longer needed. Her labour was, it seems, quite a public event. Her neighbours stood in the street waiting for progress reports throughout the labour and delivery.

❖ *Oh, they were all lined up outside, the whole street were out that day, oh, and my sister's little boy, he came knocking on't door and his mother said, 'what do you want,' and he said, 'I've brought me aunty these flowers,' and do you know what he'd done (laughs)? he'd pinched some daffodils from a garden up there, oh but it was terrible, I were in a way, and my sister's children were running wild outside, running up and down the street and they were all lined up on the other side of the street all the neighbours, there were no dinners that day for anyone.*

It seems from the storytellers' accounts, that when home births were common, it was usual to have the woman's mother and sisters present. Childless women, however (such as the woman quoted next), were not encouraged to be present during a delivery.

❖ *Well, no, I was single, you see, when my sisters had their children, so I wasn't there. It was those who had children. I had no children so I wasn't there, I never saw it, you know.*

Romanticising the past can be very dangerous and this danger is especially great, I feel, with regard to home deliveries. Given the ways in which childbirth has been medicalised today, it can be all to easy to talk fondly of the good old days when women had their children at home. The older women who took part in this study had a very balanced attitude toward the subject of home births. They recognised that there are advantages and disadvantages associated with home deliveries. Some of the older storytellers spoke of women they had known who had died in childbirth when home deliveries were common.

❖ *I had a friend, she come to be having this baby and everything seemed alright. It seemed like a healthy pregnancy, and I'll never*

*forget, she was passing this day, and she was big, with
pregnancy, and she looked the picture of health, the absolute
picture of health, and the day after that she was dead, she'd died
having this baby. Oh, it was terribly sad, she was only a young
woman. I always felt that wouldn't have happened today, it was
some problem, some complication on the last minute, and I've
often thought to myself, when it got as they were watching you
proper, if she'd have had the benefits of all that, I bet she'd be
alive today, because it was a regular thing then, you know,
women dying with their babies.*

Some of the storytellers, however, felt that medicine had taken over
too much, and that childbirth has become objectified in the nineties.

❖ *But I think they overdo it a bit today. I mean, its a natural
thing for a woman to have a baby. Now they have them wired
up to all these machines. Well, I don't think that works, but I do
think they overdo it . . . I can't understand why they make all
this fuss, because I think it's a natural thing for a grown woman
to have a baby. If you go for your check-ups like you are
supposed to do, keep an eye on them, but you don't need all
these things showing you the baby, I don't see the point in it,
and there's no telling the effects it could be having on the baby,
but, there again, you don't hear of many babies dying now.*

Once a mother had completed her two weeks stay in bed, she could
often be back at work fairly quickly, sometimes when the baby was only
a few weeks old. It is difficult to draw any conclusions from the interviews
conducted for this study, of how long married women went on working
in Bolton. Of the older women in their eighties (seven in all) only one
reported leaving work once she became a mother. Many of the remaining
storytellers had worked in the mill full time until their retirement and they
spoke of other married women who did the same. Official records of
employer and union policies might not be the best source of accurate
information of the frequency in which married women worked. Policies

regarding married women working were not always followed to the letter and rules could be bent. Two of the storytellers in their eighties at the time of interview, told me that it was the policy of most mills to stop employing a woman once she had been married a year. But if the worker was good at her job, then the rules would be manipulated in various ways so that the employee could continue working. One storyteller reported that the policy against the employment of married women could be used by employers as an excuse to get rid of a poor worker. But if the employee was a good and reliable worker then employers would use various strategies in order to ensure that the former could continue working. The system could be manipulated apparently, by employing the woman on a temporary basis (possibly paying her less) or by giving her a job as a trainer(since the married rule did not apply to trainers) or by simply ignoring the rules.

What is clear from the storytellers' accounts is that there were more married than single women working in the mills during and after the War years. By the late sixties there were hardly any single women in the mills at all. In general the storytellers interviewed in this study were in favour of a married woman working if it was practical for her to do so.

> ❖ *I'm one of these who thinks it's better for a woman to work if she wants to, they should be allowed to work, because they have a lot to offer you see, so if they want to work and they can make domestic arrangements so that they can I think they should, not just from the money angle, but they have something to give, and it keeps them alive, it keeps them in contact with current affairs. If a woman stays at home all day looking after children I'm sure she must get terribly bored, oh, I'm sure she must. Of course, some women do like to stay at home, and if they do that's OK, but if they want to work then I don't think that any obstacle should be put in their way.*

But working on a full or part time basis must have been very hard, especially for the older group who had no labour saving devices to help to lighten housework during the early years of their marriage. The storytellers, when discussing housework seemed to be very conscious of hygiene

but did not seem to consider a tidy house to be terribly important —
strangely enough a clean step was. An unscrubbed step, even in my early
married days (early seventies) was considered to be the hallmark of a slut
in Bolton. But with regard to the interiors of houses, some of the storytellers
commented on the 'unlived in,' appearance of young peoples' houses in the
nineties. One storyteller in particular considered that the present day emphasis on the ideal home, has led to people creating houses which are, in
her view, unsuitable for children. This storyteller boasted of her dining table,
which she described as so scruffy and scratched that there was no need to
worry about children making a mess of it. The table she argued, could
always be made to look nice in the event of people calling by placing a clean
table cloth on it. But for everyday living, the table's dilapidated condition
led to it being the centre of activity in the house, especially at night.

Before the introduction of the television it seems the table had been
a very important part of family life. Most working class households had
a table, in the centre of the living room or behind the couch and family
members would gather around it for meals, to gossip, to sew, embroider
or read. Prior to households having electricity an oil lamp was placed on
the centre of the table so that this was the only place in the room where
people could see to do anything at night.

People who were affluent enough to have a parlour usually had a
special polished top table in that room. This was treasured and protected.
But the everyday table was usually quite a battered old thing. Two of the
storytellers made very negative comments about the tables people have
in the house in the nineties. These, they argued, are too nice for *real* family
living. What a family needs they argued was an old battered table around
which families can enjoy hobbies without the fear of marking the wood-
work. Although tidiness in itself does not appear to have had any great
value, cleanliness of the home and of individual bodies was considered
to be of the utmost importance.

❖ *Children, it was always considered, should be bathed everyday.
It was really considered to be very important to give them this
daily bath. I've seen women with seven children, and those*

children still got a bath everyday, I think this had come about because there was disease you see, and a lot of children actually died in those days through these infectious diseases because there was so many people living together, so there was a lot of fear amongst parents that their children would get them, not just things like diphtheria, but skin disease as well, so parents were very keen to bath their children every day.

Attention to personal hygiene, may have been quite difficult because few houses had bathrooms. For children and sometimes adults, tin baths were used. The storytellers who gave descriptions of the tin bath suggested that it could be quite cosy, bathing in front of the fire. However, filling the bath, with water boiled in copper kettles and emptying it, was hard work. One storyteller left hers outside. This mistake was to cause the flooding of her living room floor because the bottom of the bath, which had rusted, came away with the weight of her body. People could also use the local slipper baths which were greatly treasured by the local workers, some of whom called in on their way home from work.

❖ *There used to be some at Clarence Street and at Moss Street, and they had baths and a wash house as well, you could take all your washing. We had no baths then so every Saturday we used to go down there. There was some on the High Street as well, I remember there was a councillor, he fought for them and they were lovely little baths, nice and low, the others were old-fashioned big ones, but these were just nice. I worked for a time at Edges (The Dolly Blue firm) and you got full of dye, your clothes, your feet, and your hair were full of this dye. When you washed your hair it used to come out a nice stony red sometimes, it was a nice colour really, and all your clothes were full of dye, so we used to call there on our way home from work, and it was cheap; well, it would have cost you as much to be boiling all that water at home, and you could fill these up, oh, you could have as much hot water as you liked. Oh, it was smashing, it was a nice way to end the day, we used to come straight out of work and into those baths.*

The wash house was also very useful to the local people. Some of the storytellers reported a preference for washing their clothes at home in a dolly tub (until the early fifties when washing machines became available). The washing was hung outside in the back streets on dry days, or in the kitchen on a wooden clothes line if it rained. There were two types of clothes-line used in the home. One was the stand up wooden maiden. Another type was made up of four poles and was suspended from the kitchen ceiling or over the living room fire. These maidens were very useful but they were gradually replaced by electric dryers and tidy drys. It is the opinion of the writer that these modern contraptions are in many ways inferior to the old clothes lines. Electric dryers fill your house with heat and steam. The string of the modern tidy dry lacks the strength of wood so that washing is forever touching the floor. It could be argued that we took a step back when we modernised our homes and removed the wooden clothes dryers. One sight which has disappeared from Bolton life is that of rows and rows of washing in the backstreets on washdays. It is ironic that at a time when people are much better off financially (and this is not to deny that there is still a lot of poverty) that we are afraid to put our washing out in public in case it gets stolen. Those who did use the local wash house could take advantage of modern technology and have all their clothes and linen taken care of in one session.

> ❖ *It was part of Moss Street Baths, it was on the other side, and a friend of mine would rather go there than wash at home. She said, 'there's always lots of hot water.' She was always asking me to go, and I never went, she was always saying there was lots of hot water. Well, it was difficult for us because we only had little boilers in the kitchen, and then there were these big machines what you could put sheets and pillow slips on you know, and they would be nice and flat when you came out, and I must say her washing was beautiful. There were a lot of people who used the wash house, and they preferred it to washing at home.*

In addition to the convenience and the facilities of the wash houses the visit was a social event as well. Although none of the storytellers interviewed in this study used the wash house, they all gave glowing accounts of it based on the information they gathered from those who went. Some visitors to the wash houses took flasks and a packet of cigs along with them. They could enjoy a smoke, a drink and a chat with some of their friends whilst waiting for the washing cycle to be completed.

❖ *Oh, yes, a friend of mine went and she used to enjoy it, they used to have big prams, you know, those that went to the wash house, they used to get these old prams, it might have even been their own old pram. Now, there was a woman I knew, she was a real decent hard-working woman, and she had a real hard life because her husband was a boozer and he used to knock her about. Well, she loved that trip to the wash house, she could meet up with people she knew and have a chat, oh, she used to really look forward to the trip to the wash house. She said it kept her sane, that, going down there for a chat.*

A little sachet of blue dye, the Dolly Blue was used for whites.

❖ *Dolly Blue, oh, yes, now let me tell you the story of the Dolly Blue man. It was an elderly man that lived in Halliwell some where round Raphael Street I think, and you know how older people used to wash in the sink, there was no washing machines then, and they wanted something to get their clothes white, and this old man he thought it up himself, he got this like Dolly blue stuff and it was like a little blue ball, and there was paper round. He was called Edge, so they called it 'Edge's Dolly Blue', he patented it, then they couldn't take it off him, and then one day a women said, 'it would be better if you could put something in this because you get all blue on your fingers,' so he invented the little Dolly Blue stick, a little stick like that and you could dip the stick in your wash without touching the blue, and that was the latest Dolly Blue. You don't see those now, and then he invented the Dolly Blue cream for creaming curtains and that. Of course, he's dead now, years ago, and he made a fortune out of that.*

The storytellers all spoke of the poverty of their youth. Working class women had to be skilled cooks and housekeepers in order to make meagre wages stretch to feed and clothe their families. The striking thing about the accounts (given by the older storytellers especially) is of how every ounce of food was used in order to maximise its nutritional value for the family. Bones were boiled to make stock for gravy and broths. Dough was made up and one half used for the making of bread while the other half had currants added to make scones and tea cakes. Porridge was served for breakfast, half an egg or pobbs, bread and milk served in a pint pot. Rhubarb was a big hit in Bolton until fairly recent times. Rhubarb was cheap to buy, but if people had a piece of land (no matter how small) they would grow their own. Stewed or baked in a pie, rhubarb was a popular filler after a first course. Rhubarb was also good for the bowels; there was once a time when being 'regular' was considered to be as important (if not more so) than the cleaning of teeth.

❖ *When you got up in the morning you'd just have a jam butty or something like that, but when you come home for your dinner your mam would have cooked you some potato pie, or a meat and potato pie, and you'd get a dish like that (indicates size). There'd be potatoes, carrots, peas, dripping, we always used to put dripping on it and water and honest, me mam could make a dinner out of one piece of meat. You only got half a pound of pieces and before we went to school she'd say, 'just nip down to the butchers and get a pound of pieces,' and you'd go down and the butcher would gather all the pieces for you, and cut them all up and you could be getting some of the best meat in those pieces, and pieces then you got for three pence a pound. Then she'd say, 'go and get a marrow bone,' and you got a marrow bone and that went in and then she'd make a big rice pudding. When you the came home you'd have potatoes pie or potato hash, a pan of dumplings, or she'd get a ham bone, she'd get a cabbage, she'd put a ham bone and cabbage in, and then, oh, sorry, it were spare ribs and cabbage, and she'd get a ham shank and she'd fill it with peas, lentils and barley, you had that. Then for your tea she used to buy rock salmon and she used to make flour and cook that and you'd get a big slice with chips and bread and flour cakes. She used to bake them and then on Friday that were a treat she used to get us vanillas, and she used to get faded fruit and cut the faded out and make pies out of that.*

The account given above is fairly typical of descriptions given by the interviewees of the skills of working class mothers. Although people were poor, it is clear that mothers were very keen to ensure that their families were well nourished. A little of something was considered to be better than nothing at all. Several storytellers told of how their mothers would break a couple of fruits into segments to be divided between the whole family. In this way, each family member got a little fruit even if they did not get a whole one. Fruit was considered to be very important for people's health, especially those which were in season (out of season fruits were too expensive since they had to be imported or grown under glass). If you missed having at least one serving of a fruit in season, it was believed that your health would suffer. This belief probably had much to commend it. There is nothing in the older women's stories to suggest that people knew anything about vitamins, and yet mothers seemed to have an intuitive knowledge that fruit was good for your health. The diet of many working class families prior to the Second World War does seem to have been very high in fats and carbohydrates. One of the older storyteller's commented on this remarking that the women of her youth tended to be somewhat stockier than the average woman of today. This was not considered to be a problem, however, because several of the storytellers reported that men preferred a woman with a bit of flesh on her in the early years of the century. In the older women's youth it was considered healthy to be a little on the large size, especially with regard to a woman's ability to have children. The storyteller who had the difficult labour at home for example *(see page 70)* attributed her problems to the fact that she was very slim which had been unusual for women in her youth.

The fat content of meals was probably increased because mothers, in their efforts to increase the nutritional value of a plate of chips or potatoes, poured broth or gravy made from stock over the meal. This stock was soaked up with bread and dripping. The older women interviewed however, were all in their eighties and do not seem to have suffered any long term ill effects from the fat consumed at meal times. It may be that any potential ill effects caused by eating so much fat may have been balanced off by the calories the women burned off in their working and family lives. Given the low budgets working class mothers had to cope with, it seems that they fed their families extremely well. It could well be the case that young women of today are less able to cope with poverty because they do not have the cooking skills of their fore sisters. Many of the recipes discussed by the older women have been forgotten, or they tend to be remembered as little more than a quaint memory of the past.

Although poverty was widespread in the storytellers youth, so was charity. There was, however, a stigma attached to accepting charity. In order to avoid stigmatising those recieving charity, those giving it would do everything possible to avoid making it clear that this was what they were doing.

❖ *There would always be the old lady who, knowing someone who was really poor would say something like, 'oh love, will you have a bit of this bacon, I keep thinking I've still got a family you know,' and so she would (the housewife) get some bacon or whatever, but they would cover up whenever they could the fact that they were giving charity to save her pride. It was all kind of, 'oh, I've bought too much or, oh this is a lovely little dress and my little girl's only had it five minutes, will you take it? I can't bear to throw it out,' and all this sort of thing, so that she could save face. Children, if they saw a poorer child in a dress that they knew their mother had given to their mother, they would never mention it, they would never say to other children, 'oh my mother gave her that dress,' there was this unspoken rule, to give people as much dignity as possible in their poverty.*

The stories told by the women who took part in this study suggest that although there was still a lot of poverty around in the fifties, standards of living were gradually improving. The breakfast time pobbs, porridge or jam butty had been replaced with cereals. The bucket of water used to keep milk fresh and the meat safe (a cupboard with a meshed front for keeping meat) were gradually replaced with the modern fridge. Electric washers had become a standard feature in most kitchens, although the early washers had to be filled using a hose pipe connected to a tap and emptied via a bucket underneath. By the fifties many women owned a hoover or a ewbank, a sort of imitation hoover with brushes inside which rotated when you pushed it. Even in the fifties however, carpets and rugs were often placed outside on a line and given a good beating to get rid if the dust. Women were still doing a lot of home cooking and baking until very recent years — in the fifties this was usually done on an electric or gas cooker since many people were having the red ranger (a fireplace with a built in cooker) removed and having their fire places modernised. Indeed, we frequently reminisce about the wonderful cooks mothers once were, but we tend to forget that there are a lot of keen cooks around today.

CHAPTER SIX

WOMEN IN THE UNIONS

I had been working in the mill for about a month and I wasn't happy about my wage. I was sixteen and people of my age didn't get full pay — we got half. I was working just as hard and producing just as much. So I spoke to my mother about it — I said that I was going to protest. My mum and her mates agreed with me. We discussed the matter over the morning tea break sitting on tin cans — the ones that left a red mark around your bum.

It was decided. I would approach the boss and complain. The hour of confrontation was set for 2 p.m. that afternoon. The appointed hour came. The boss, a smart middle aged man could be seen talking to the crealers. My legs seemed quite wobbly — I seemed to have lost all the confidence I'd had that morning when I'd complained about the wage packet. I thought for a moment about getting out of it. I tried to avoid eye contact with my mother who was now looking in my direction with an expectant expression on her face. Damn her! Why did she have to bring us up to stick up for ourselves? Well . . . it was becoming clear as the hand of the clock rested on ten past two that I wasn't going to get out of this. I'd blabbed too much in the morning break and now all eyes were on me — waiting.

I put my knotter down (the instrument used to piece up yarn) nodded to my mother, her mate, her mate, everybody's mate, brassed myself and approached the enemy.

'Please Sir.' I put up my hand. Hell! Why did I do that? I'm not at school. He'll know I'm nervous now. My hand shot down as quickly as I'd raised it and I placed it firmly behind my back, holding it with my other hand on order to prevent myself from making the same mistake again. As a matter of fact he was very nice about it, the boss. He was clearly amused at me putting up my hand like that and as I talked he was trying hard to suppress a smile. I told him about my wage and of how I disagreed with being paid less just because of my age. Logical argument — I'd learnt all about that at the art college when we'd had those debates about abortion, Bob Dylan and a woman's right to work. Don't lose your cool (don't put up your hand). Give your argument in a straightforward way. Respect the point of view of the other person even if you disagree with it. I stated my case, ending by giving the boss my assurance that since he was clearly an honest and reasonable man (was he?) I felt confident that he would see my point of view and do the *right* thing — pay me the full rate. 'OK — get lost and I'll think about it' he said, or words to that effect. I walked back to frame, even taller. I nodded at my mum, her mate, everybody's mate and carried on work. The following week I received full pay in my wage packet.

This way of dealing with disagreements was fairly typical in the mill and reflects a form of interpersonal behaviour described by a psychologist called Carol Gilligan. Gilligan was to show that the moral thinking of women is different from that of men. Men's morality is characterised by autonomy and the application of abstract, objective principles such as that of justice. But women's morality contrasts with this and is characterised by the need to avoid hurt, to maintain relationships whenever possible and a strong sense of connectedness with others.

Gilligan's model I feel, can be used to explain the behaviour of men and women in the mills with regard to union matters because relationships tend to be important to working-class people.

Despite my mother's involvement in the union when she worked in the mill, her advice to me when I complained about my pay was to see the boss first. Her advice reflected a concern for feelings and for maintaining relationships in the workplace, a desire to settle the matter if possible by drawing on interpersonal skills. In this way the boss was given the opportunity to think about the unfair practice of paying younger workers less and to change his practice without the need for mass public involvement, debate and friction. This is not to suggest that women would be content to leave things as they stood if their initial appeals were unsuccessful. My mother in fact had advised me to take my case to the unions if my confrontation with the boss proved unsuccessful. But her advice to approach him first reflects a faith in the basic goodness and fairness of people, a belief that everyone should be given the benefit of the doubt before moving on to challenge and resist. If direct appeals failed then women could be just as assertive as the men, moving a formerly private encounter into the public arena.

> ❖ *This is a funny story, but there was one woman there, she was always in unions meetings and all this kind of thing. If there was anything going on she was always involved and if the talks didn't get her anywhere, with the bosses, she'd go into the yard (laughs). It was funny, and she'd be shouting to them all, she didn't agree with this and she didn't agree with that. The bosses didn't like her for that . . . the workers liked her because she stuck up for them, she was for the workers you see, because they were working for very low wages and she'd see to anything that went wrong. She was that type of person. My husband said they were all frightened of her, the bosses because she wouldn't just go to see them and leave it at that. Oh, no, she'd be out in the yard, she'd come out with it and they didn't like it, stirring up trouble for them.*

The accounts given during the interviews for this study suggest however, that as long as bosses were responsive to the appeals made by the workers the women were content not to be too militant. This was more noticeable in the accounts given by the older women than the younger group. Two of the women in the older group for example had worked in a mill where the majority of the workers did not belong to a union at all. According to these women, the owner of the mill in question always went along with whatever the unions and other mill owners had agreed to at the end of a dispute. Therefore, as far as these mill workers were concerned there was no real need to get involved in union action. The arrangement was agreeable to both employers and employees because the former did not suffer a loss of production due to strikes and the latter did not lose wages. But the workers still reaped the benefits won for the workers by the unions.

It could be argued that such an arrangement was unfair because these workers were benefiting from a union they did not themselves support. But it is also easy to understand that in times of hardship, workers would want to avoid going on strike if possible. Therefore, the writer feels that caution should be used before criticising such behaviour, especially by those who have not experienced the hardships encountered by the women who took part in this study.

One of the women who had worked in the mill described above did contribute to the unions. In other words, the woman contributed to the unions financially but did not support them by going on strike when there was a dispute. She explained that she made the payments to the unions, partly because she believed it to be the right thing to do The storyteller's belief that she might at some time need the unions proved to be correct because she did have a disagreement with her employers about her wages at one point in her working life.

❖ *There were different strengths of yarn, some were silk, some were cotton, some were cotton and wool . . . well, if you had all silk on your frames you got more money than anyone else because it were for parachutes. Well, I were in't union, I were the only one that were in and I'd never told anyone that I were in. This time they'd changed me frames onto all silk. Well, with having that on I should have got more wages than anyone else . . . well, I got me wages. but I only got my wage for what I'd been on before they never paid me for the silk, so I told them, I went to the boss and told him I wanted paying for the silk. Well, he said that there was nobody else bothered because they weren't in't unions you see, so they could do what they wanted*

*with them ... I said I wanted paying for me silk, you see, and he
said I couldn't have it, so I said I was going to the union
(laughs). I got my silk.*

During her interview the woman quoted above insisted that she
worked for a good firm but she also acknowledged that even 'good'
employers would, if they could, take advantage of their workers. But the
workers who did not join the union, whether male or female, were the
exception rather than the rule.

During the course of the interviews, I was very privileged to meet an
older woman who had actually worked with the union, an ex weaver. This
woman was fascinating to talk to. As a union worker, she had travelled
the world and she had spoken publicly on many occasions, as a Christian
and as a union official. This storyteller viewed her union responsibilities
from a Christian perspective.

❖ *You may get a few bad apples (in the union) but I can tell
you about trade union secretaries who were members of the
Salvation Army. I, myself, am a religious person, and I know the
secretary of the local card room was a devout Roman Catholic,
and yet to listen to these politicians we are all corrupt, we are
all bad. Well, we certainly wasn't. You might get the one bad
apple, but not generally, we are peace-loving people, all we did
was for the best for the workers, your members paid you and you
just did your best for them.*

From the extract of transcript quoted above it is clear that this storyteller could not separate her Christianity from her role as a Trades Union
Secretary. She went on to say:

❖ *I loved it, yes, I did (her work in the unions), and I look back
on it with pleasure now, and I loved our members. Obviously they
had their failings like anyone else, but I loved them for all their
failings, I still loved them and I would do all I could for them.*

It was clear from the conversation I enjoyed with this woman, that she could be a person to be reckoned with. She was a keen believer in equal rights for women who, during the course of her working life had done much to protect the interests of her members. Her talk reflected a deep understanding for the life situations of the women she represented, so that her feminism was not of the middle class professional but of the working class woman. She recognised for example that the nuclear family, headed by a male bread winner and promoted as the norm in Western society was far from a reality for many women working in the mills. She knew that many of her members were divorced, separated or for various other reasons, the main breadwinner of the family. This understanding was to lead her to resist any policies based on assumptions about the nuclear family.

❖ *Redundancies. I had some battles because sometimes it would be argued that the married women should be the first to go, you see, and I used to argue, 'no we can't do that because you don't know the circumstances of that married woman, she might be the only bread winner, she may be separated from her husband.' No-one knows unless you start asking them, and I didn't go around asking them, although they very often told me, so we agreed to a policy of part timers and last in first out, but I would not agree to the policy of married women first. Sometimes it caused a row, but I stuck to my guns about that.*

This union storyteller, along with her other colleagues was to resist the introduction of a policy to have women work nights in the mills, despite pressure from the Equal Opportunities Commission. But the philosophy of equal opportunities as designed by middle class professional people does not take into account the physical, social and economic constraints which apply to masses of people whose lives are ruled by more important considerations (for them) than utopian theories. In this way, egalitarian principles when forced into practice often present people with dilemmas they cannot cope with. In the context referred to here, if women in the mills had been forced to work nights then this could have led to terrible financial and practical problems for some women, especially single parents. Any policy claiming to represent Equal Opportunities which fails to recognise that women's experience of work is very different from men's leads to the continued exploitation of women rather than their empowerment. This is a point which the union storyteller clearly understood.

> ❖ *They were asking women to go on night work. There was a*
> *history to that because we'd always been opposed to women*
> *working at night. We accepted them working in the hospitals and*
> *all that but not in the mills because we didn't see that it was*
> *necessary. It had always been the case that men had worked at*
> *night and women worked the double day shift, and we upheld*
> *that policy until the Equal Opportunities caught up with us and*
> *they made it clear to us that if we weren't prepared to let the*
> *women work nights they would take us to the European Court,*
> *but it was going to break out into a big row, so we got the*
> *women together and asked them what they wanted us to do*
> *because after all they were the ones who would be affected by it,*
> *and the result was that they would agree to work nights as long*
> *as they wasn't pressurised into doing it . . . so it came to be the*
> *policy that women could work nights but they had not to be*
> *compelled to do so. But I had a big headache about that, I gave a*
> *paper on it in Amsterdam and I had to give in to it. It was a*
> *big headache, losing all your principles.*

In the extract of transcript quoted above there is further evidence that women tended to deal with matters directly and collectively, taking into account the needs and views of the workers while at the same time trying to find an agreement which would be acceptable to all. Rather than involve herself and the union in a conflict with the Equal Opportunities Commission, the woman appealed to the workers to tell her what they wanted her to do. In this way she was able to come to a compromise. In order to reach this compromise the woman had to sacrifice many of her own principles for what she considered to be the greater good, this being the knowledge that she was doing the best she could for her members while at the same time avoiding an expensive and costly battle involving the

European court. It is not argued here that men in the unions always took an aggressive approach whereas women did not. The argument offered here, is that women in their union activities may have been more likely to avoid conflict if they could, in the same way that they tend to be the peace makers and pacifists of their own homes.

The union storyteller was in no way hesitant to mobilise her union members into union action if necessary. But she nonetheless demonstrated in her talk a preference for dealing with disputes by drawing on her interpersonal skills if possible.

There were many times during her interview that the union storyteller spoke of approaching the employers personally, or by letter or phone in order to ensure that the rights of worker were respected. She told of one worker who, on retirement, was refused her pension. The reason given for this refusal was that the woman had on one occasion (many years before her retirement) walked out after an argument at work. When she returned to work a few days later no one mentioned the incident but when the woman came to retire she was refused her pension on the grounds that she had broken her service. When the storyteller heard of the retired worker's problems she wrote a sharp letter of protest to the retired worker's former employer. This proved to be successful because the woman got her pension after all. It seemed from the union storyteller's discussion that many of the employers had tremendous respect for her as well and she spoke at great length of the satisfactory relationships she enjoyed with some of the mill owners and managers. Two former managers in fact still keep in touch with her by letter and phone.

There were times, the union storyteller admitted when direct appeals to the employers did not help matters. But even on occasions such as this, she was willing to bide her time and wait until she had the cards on her side. She would then use this bargaining power in order to get her way at a later date. And despite her generally good relationship with the employers this woman was far from naive about their ability to exploit the workers. One of her greatest criticisms of the present times was that employers have far too much of their own way because the unions have lost so much power.

❖ *They have no bargaining power (the workers), and people are*
having to put up with all sorts which really they wouldn't have to
do if trade were good . . . because they are frightened to speak out
now, they are afraid of complaining in case it leads to the loss of
their jobs in some indirect way, but if and when we revert back to
full trade, it will happen again, it's just not on the side of the
unions at the moment, it's the employers getting all their own way.

A popular political argument in recent years has been that we should revert back to Victorian principles. The important question to ask with regard to such an ideal is, which Victorian principles are we talking about? The pro Victorian discourse seems to be very much against the unions and yet the union storyteller was in her mid eighties at the time of her interview and she remembers that the workers of her youth were much more involved in the unions than people tend to be in the nineties. It would therefore appear that the Victorian principles advocated by right-wing ideologists are strictly to do with the way that governments should rule rather than the way that the general working population should think. For if the working class population of this country were to adopt the 'Victorian principles' of their forebears then they would be actively organising themselves into unions, as the textile workers involved in this study did, following the examples of their parents and grandparents.

Trades Unions organised by men however did not always work with the interests of women in mind as the interview with the union storyteller made clear. One cause of conflict between the sexes in the mills came about because of the introduction of ring spinning. Prior to the introduction of ring spinning the mills had employed the use of the Spinning Mule invented by Samuel Crompton. Mule spinning was very well paid and a prestigious occupation in the mills and this was a male occupation. Ring spinning was to be a woman's occupation. The Mule Spinners' union was to put up a great deal of resistance against the introduction of ring spinning because this threatened the mens powerful position in the mills. The Mule Spinners' union as a part of their resistance were to exclude women from joining their ranks. This was a strategy which was to backfire on them.

❖ *The Mule Spinners, they were the aristocrats, and they were
all male and they were really the well off people of the trade as
you might say. In my way of thinking, they made a big mistake
because, when the firm introduced ring spinning, it took the
place of Mule spinning. At that time the Mule spinners
wouldn't let women into the unions, they always felt that mule
spinning would go on for ever and there would always be men
doing Mule spinning you see, but it didn't work like that
because ring spinning came big. The women were able to do ring
spinning you see and so they put the women on the rings and
the men wouldn't accept them and eventually the mules went
out and with them going out, so did the Mule spinning union
which was male dominated. They were the king-pins of the
spinning industry. They didn't bother us because we were on the
weaving side but they were the wealthy people and they hardly
ever left and the poor little piecer or cross piecer had to wait
until some one left or died before they could get on the Mules.*

Women had equal pay along with the men in the textile industry. But
not all of the women who took part in this study felt supportive of the
unions. One storyteller in particular felt that union officials were far too
friendly with the bosses and therefore did very little (in her view) to
challenge the abuse and exploitation of the workers. Some of the storytellers also commented that the women in the textile industry had a very
instrumental attitude towards the unions, only supporting them when
they needed some help themselves. The storytellers who made comments
such as this, however, said that they considered that this instrumental
attitude workers had towards the unions to be quite typical and it was
this they believed which had led to the present powerlessness of the
unions.

❖ *Well, they couldn't care less one way or another (the workers)
unless it affected them, and then they would often go and see to
it themselves, like I did when I wasn't getting any extra money.
There was none of them would back me up though.*

But people's attitudes towards the unions, as with all things in life, would be inclined to vary. Within any union there will be people who will become members for a variety of different reasons. And how many people who are union members can really put their hands on their hearts and say that there is not at least some self interest involved in their membership? Even the older woman who took part in this study who joined the union because she believed it was the right thing to do, also admitted that she had been partly motivated by the possibility that she might need the unions at some stage.

There were practical constraints which prevented some women from being as involved in the unions as they would like to have been, a point made by some of the storytellers when asked if women were very involved in the unions.

> ❖ *Not as much as the men, we used to go to the meetings that we could manage, and I used to know a woman (she's ninety-two now, and she's in a nursing home) who used to go to all the union meetings, and read all the books. She used to go to the spinners' hall to all the meetings. She was very active in the unions, I didn't really go as much as I would like to have done but its very difficult when you've got young children, it's very hard to be as involved as you would like to be, but a lot were . . . they tended to be the unmarried ones.*

Working full time, attending to children and housework would understandably restrict women's attendance at union meetings. In the case of the older group, the strict moral conduct demanded of women which led to them in their youth spending most evenings at home would no doubt have restricted their ability to attend meetings as well. But despite all the restrictions imposed on women's lives during the heyday of the textile industry, it does seem that they went out of their way to be involved in the unions. Indeed, in view of their everyday constraints, women it could be argued, were as committed (if not more) to their unions as the men.

Little piecers and cross piecers were young boys (paid by the spinners) who pieced up broken threads to the yarn so that the spinning would not be interrupted.

CHAPTER SEVEN

THE NIGHT THEY BOMBED MANCHESTER

The adults had been through this War, walked right through it. They told me so. That was before I was here. I got born you see and before that I wasn't here. I can remember thinking about this fact (which was something of a revelation to me) that there had been a time when I did not exist — I could not imagine a world without me in it. But there it was, the grown ups had assured me that there had been such a time, before I got this thing called 'born'.

The adults told us all about this War, especially the Grandads. Grandads were people who, when you talked to other kids were boring because they always talked about the War. Privately they were interesting because they did just that. I knew the War had been important. Lots of people were still talking about the War when I was a child. But as a child I could never really grasp what war was about. I certainly did not have any understanding of death, although I had started to think about it and decided that being dead must be the same as not being born — you were not here, the world was back to being without you.

War is something which adults and children perceive in very different ways. It seems from the interviews conducted for this study that the storytellers who experienced war as children did not have a much more realistic perception than I had done when, as a little girl I had listened to stories about it. To an adult, war is a serious business no matter how far away the battles are being fought. To a child, unable to grasp an understanding of concepts such as death, war is a much more exciting affair. It is a 'thing,' saturated with adventure, sometimes arousing a morbid curiosity. The older storytellers had experienced both the First and Second World Wars. The accounts they gave reflect two very different perceptions about what war is all about — one of a child, another as an adult. During the interviews, it often seemed that when the storytellers spoke of their experiences they appeared to relive them as well, entering the perceptual consciousness of their former self. So when telling stories of childhood memories people become for a time, children again. The childhood memories of war reveal it as extraordinary, an event, such as this story of the zeppelin given by a woman in her eighties.

❖ *Well, I remember when we saw a zeppelin, my sister across the street, your Grandma and myself . . . and we slept in the back room. It were when t' War were on and me Dad was in the Royal Marines, he were in France, my Dad. Anyway, me Mother came out from front room, and she said, 'leave that light alone and don't touch it,' she said, 'there's a zeppelin over, there's a zeppelin.' We never touched the light, but we went to the back bedroom window, and we drew curtains back and it were just passing this zeppelin, and it were a big basket underneath and it were a big long one going like that, proper slow like that.'*

This account is very atmospheric. It somehow captures not only the awe and excitement which the family must have experienced to witness such an event but also the intimacy of family relationships. There is a saying that war draws people together and it would seem from many of the things the storytellers said during the interviews that this saying is very true. Stories such as the one cited above, however, reflect this sense of sharing, of how people in war reach out to each other, not only in times of trouble but in order to share unique experiences such as this as well. One feels when reading the account of the zeppelin that it was all the more exciting because the characters in the scenario were sharing it with each other.

The zeppelin indicated the presence of a danger which was very real because it was floating across the sky with the intention of bombing the railway station in Bolton town centre. Richardson's book, 'Zeppelins over Lancashire,' (1992) gives a graphic account of the loss of property and life in Bolton at the time of its passing. The account of the devastation described in Richardson's book was mentioned to the storyteller quoted above during the interview and she was very surprised to hear of it. Apparently, the news of the bombings had not reached her when she was a child, so that she had spent her eighty six years totally unaware of the devastation the zeppelin had caused. It is difficult to speculate as to why the older woman had been unaware of the bombings. Had the adults of her world protected her, fearing that news of the bombings may have frightened her? Had she forgotten? Or had the bombings been swallowed up and rendered insignificant in a swamp of war memories? What is clear is that to this older woman and her sisters, the appearance of the zeppelin had been an exciting experience and nothing more. The woman insisted that she, her mother and sisters were not frightened by the sight of the zeppelin at all. Indeed, the excitement caused by the zeppelin was so overwhelming that the family completely forgot all safety regulations and they threw back the curtains in order to catch a clear view of it.

❖ *No we weren't (frightened). It were something you never thought you'd see again . . . we weren't supposed to (open the curtains) but we did because we'd have no light in . . . because we were watching it I wonder how many could say that, they'd seen that zeppelin going over . . . we saw it.*

Fear of death was overcome by curiosity, the need to capture history in motion. How sophisticated of such young children (this woman was about eight years old when she saw the zeppelin going over) to realise that this was a future story they could tell — grab it while you can, history in the making. The woman's narrative did, however, reflect some recognition of the zeppelin's potential danger because she admitted that she knew it was carrying bombs but did not really think about it very much at the time.

❖ *Yes, that's what they were coming for, that's what they were doing, but you see, they didn't drop any round here (bombs).*

Out of sight, out of mind — the reality of bombing was recognised but pushed to the back of consciousness. To another woman who was also a child witness of the zeppelins crossing, the event was remembered quite differently because this women had lived near the area in which the bombings took place. Her recollection of the zeppelin was one of horror.

❖ *I remember the zeppelin and the air raid. They dropped about four bombs on Plodder Lane. They were looking for Trinity Street station and the church is near . . . and where the church is now, there was a row of houses and they just overlapped what they were going for . . . and the bombs dropped on the houses and killed an awful lot of people.*

When asked what her first impressions of the zeppelin were, the woman cited above answered that she found the experience:

❖ *Frightening, very frightening . . . you didn't know what to expect.*

The conversations about the War which emerged during the interviews suggest that it can be very difficult to grasp the reality of war unless it is part of their lived experience. The two very different accounts of the zeppelin illustrate this point. Both of the women cited witnessed the passing of the zeppelin. For one of the women, it was an exciting event which would provide her with an interesting tale to tell. But the second woman who had lived near the devastation the zeppelin left behind recalled the incident as a traumatic and horrifying experience.

But as many of the storytellers pointed out, the First World War had been fought in the trenches, far away. So, for the young people at least, war provided a host of adventurous stories. These war stories were of particular interest when they were told by those heroes who had actually been there. Wounded soldiers who had been shipped home to convalesce provided younger and old alike with a wealth of information about the War.

❖ *Watermillock, that were a home for wounded soldiers. When we were coming home from school, there were soldiers who had been wounded, some with their arms in slings, some with bandaged*

heads, some with stiff legs, and they used to have to report round
the Lamb Hotel (Halliwell Road). They used to have two forms
there, for the soldiers at Watermillock, and they used to come out
of Watermillock, and they used to sit on these forms They were in
grey and blue flannelette suits . . . because they used to speak to
us going to school, they'd be talking, and that's how we learnt all
about the War, you know, talking to these soldiers.

No matter how explicit the war stories told by the soldiers may have
been, it is unlikely that such information will have given children a realistic
impression of what it was like. For one older storyteller (86 at the time
of interview in 1988) who has since died, war meant that she had to be
separated from her childhood sweetheart. This young man was only
eighteen years of age when he had been called up to fight. The couple
had known each other for many years prior to their courtship and they
were very eager to get married before the young man went to war.

❖ *I'd loved him from being a little girl, I were fourteen, he were*
sixteen, we played together, I lived in that street and he lived
just at the back . . . then we started going together, then he went
in the army, and he came over, and it were a Khaki wedding,
and we started courting, I were just fourteen then, just fourteen.
We were married on the Saturday, and we had a coach and four
white horses . . . and my Dad said, 'you're doing well, a coach
and four white horses, and that's how we were married. Oh, it
was beautiful . . . and then I never saw him again till about 8
months later when he came home.

A coach and four white horses may seem an unnecessary expense,
especially for a couple who were so short of money. But such extravagance
needs to be considered in the context of the young people's lives at the time.
This couple could not be sure that they would ever see each other again.
There would be little confidence when they took their wedding vows that
they would have the opportunity to share a life together. Is it any wonder
then, that the young man wanted to make the wedding very special,

something his bride would never forget? There was after all every possibility that this wedding memory of her husband may have been the last. In view of the circumstances, a big wedding may have seemed important to the couple's parents. Luckily for this couple, the young man survived the war and lived a long and happy life. But there were many other young brides who became war widows. Other wives welcomed home from the war husbands who were so traumatised that they bore little resemblance to the young men they said goodbye to only a few years before.

The Second World War

When the storytellers spoke of the Second World War, many gave an account of a spectacular bombing. It is difficult to know if the storytellers were referring to the same event when they describe the bombing, or if they were referring to different events. Unfortunately, no one could remember the dates in which the events described took place. It is unlikely however, that anyone could have missed the events described. So the writer feels that it is reasonable to assume that the storyteller's quoted below are discussing the same event which seems to outline the first bombing of the city of Manchester. Specific names and dates are irrelevant in this study anyway because it is not concerned with accurate recordings of war events but with peoples lived experiences and perceptions of them.

The bombing referred to during the interviews suggest that this was the first time people understood the dangers of war. This incident was to mark the beginning of the blitz, a period of time in the history of Bolton which was a nightmare for most people.

> ❖ *My son was born in the morning and on this day it was one of the biggest air raids here, and they pushed all our beds to the middle of the ward and put red blankets on the bottom of our beds, because you weren't allowed out of bed if you'd had your baby that day. In them days you weren't allowed up for ten days after, and they said, 'all your babies are in a safe place so don't worry about them.' For five hours they bombed the towns. Manchester and Liverpool, and every time a bomb went off it*

rattled the windows. It was very frightening and I thought, 'hell I've been through all this (the labour) and now I'm going to get bombed.' But having the baby, that was easy in comparison to that you know, even though birth in those days wasn't easy (laughs). We kept hiding under our covers. It was silly really, because what good would a blanket have done you, you'd have been blown to pieces wouldn't you? It's funny how people do that when they're frightened, but we did, we were there, all the women in this labour ward, curled up in a little ball, hiding under your blanket . . . we'd stick our heads out every now and again and talk to each other and then another would go off and the windows would rattle and we'd be there again, shivering with fear under this blanket.

❖ *I remember the night they bombed Manchester, we watched it my brother and I from the top of Merehall (an area in Bolton). Oh, it was terrible, it was a sight you'd never forget, we'd never seen anything like it. There it was all the sky ablaze, it was night, early evening and it should have been dark really, but we could see it in the distance, and the sky was lit up, lit up to blazes with this red flame, this red flame and then all white on top, and all this noise. Oh, it was tremendous this noise, like thunder it was, and I said to my friend., 'What's that, where's all that fire coming from?' and she said, 'Why haven't you heard? They are bombing Manchester.' You were frightened to death because Manchester always seemed such a long way away. It's not like it is now, you know you can nip on a train or a bus and be in Manchester in a minute, but not then . . . and I thought, oh, heck, what will happen when they get here, you know, if they can make a fire like that . . . oh, it was very frightening. I can remember that very clearly, standing on Merehall watching Manchester burn, and being really terrified really because you see, we'd never really understood till then just how much damage a bomb could do.*

The Second World War was remembered far more vividly then the first even by the older women who had experienced both. The Second World War however, was not fought solely in the trenches so that it was difficult for people to think of it in abstract terms. People found the blitz to be particularly frightening.

> ❖ *Oh, it was awful, everything was blacked out. You had to*
> *have curtains, when it was lighting up time . . . you didn't have*
> *a bit of light . . . you bought black stuff, they made black*
> *curtains, you didn't have to have a tinkle of light showing, there*
> *was no light showing, there was no light in the streets, you had*
> *to have a little torch but you had to be careful how you shone it.*

But as was the case in the stories told of the First World War, the younger you were, the less frightening war appeared to be. The younger women who took part in the study described the blitz with far less emotional feeling than those who were older. Perhaps it was a blessing that younger people did not grasp the full extent of the danger (or did they push the danger to the back of their minds). It seems from the descriptions the women gave of the home air raid shelters, that these would have offered very little safety in the event of an attack.

> ❖ *— We had a council house, and the council put air raid shelters*
> *in. Now this was a hole in the ground, to waist level and then*
> *corrugated iron above, and you kind of went in a hole. Now I only*
> *ever remember playing in that air raid shelter because my mother*
> *was too ill to be moved (this woman's mother had a terminal illness*
> *during the War from which she died) and I was too young to get*
> *myself ready and go to school, so I stayed at my grandmother's.*

When I first heard the storytellers' descriptions of shelters such as the one mentioned above I felt that they probably served no other purpose other than that of providing the family with some psychological reassurance. It is hard to imagine that it would withstand the effects of a bombing attack. However, these Anderson shelters (as I was told they were called) were very safe, especially since according to the storytellers, if outside during a bomb attack you were much more likely to be injured or killed by flying glass or a falling building. Apparently, after the War, many people used their Anderson shelters to grow mushrooms. The public shelters may have been a little safer, although how much safer it is difficult to say.

> ❖ *Now an air-raid shelter was split between two houses, it was placed half way so that it could be used by two families, and I loved going into the air raid shelters. I couldn't sleep in case those sirens went off, not knowing the seriousness of them you see, and the planes that came across had a sound. There was a sound of breaking, a continuous sound, so you might hear them first, or mostly sirens, the air-raid sirens. It was a terrible thing, it really did spell doom, it had an awful winding sound you see.*

There is a hint of fear towards the end of this account. On the one hand the storyteller speaks of the sense of pleasure and adventure at the experience of sleeping in the air raid shelter, but on the other she admits that she recognised that the sound of the planes and the siren spelt out danger. The ambivalence shown in the storyteller's account cited above is typical of the recollections of the sirens. This contradicts the view put forward earlier in this chapter, that children do not grasp the reality of war. An alternative explanation could be that the children did appreciate the dangers but they pushed the fear to the back of their minds. There were times when some of the storytellers admitted their fear, especially when reciting stories of near death experiences of their own or of other family members. The storyteller cited below for example, had just began work in the mill when war broke out. Although she had no recollections of having to take shelter during the day she admitted that she would have found such a thing very frightening because she would not have been with her family.

> ❖ *Well, I was young and gay then so it didn't bother me so much, so it didn't bother me even at night. One night I hadn't been home long and the sirens went and we all went to the shelter. I found out my sister was missing, so I went back to get her. If it had happened during the day in the mill then it would*

*have frightened me, I would have panicked then because we both
worked in different parts of the mill, and I couldn't have been
sure she was safe.*

In the home shelters at night family members could see each other
and knew therefore that everyone was safe. But if an air raid occurred
when family members were separated from each other this must have
increased people's fears considerably. There were occasional accounts
given during the interviews which suggested that children were afraid of
the war. But it also seems to be clear that children looked to the adults
of their world for reassurance. Sometimes children would ask for this
reassurance directly as the woman cited below did.

❖ *My first memory I have of the War was, I was at my
Grandmothers house and there was a lot of shouting across the
street and a lot going on. I went out and I said to this girl who
was slightly older then me, 'what are they all shouting about,
what's all the shouting about?' and she said, 'well there's
Germans going to come walking up Groves Street very soon,
because they are going to invade this country,' and I said, 'Well
what does that mean?' She said, 'Well, these German soldiers are
going to boss us about and tell us what to do, and they have
bayonets in their guns and if we don't do as we are told they
will just come and shoot us.' So I immediately felt a very strong
sense of insecurity and I thought, 'Well, surely my Dad won't
let anyone shoot me,' and my Grandad was in the house so I
went inside and I said, 'you won't let anyone shoot me will
you?' and he said,'no there's no one going to shoot you.'*

Children put their faith in adults without question. This woman's
grandfather could not in reality give his frightened granddaughter any
guarantees that she would not get shot or blown to pieces if a bomb were
dropped. He couldn't guarantee her safety any more than he could his
own. This story is rather depressing because it tempts us to ask how many
parents in Europe during the two Wars made similar promises to their

children. And how many of these one wonders have been long dead, victims of the War possibly alongside their trusting offspring.

Another approach children used to gain reassurance was to eavesdrop on adult conversations of the War, picking up on gestures, hints and the general mood.

❖ *I was only young, but something told me that what was being said on the radio was very important and I actually remember Churchill making his speech, not so much what he said, but the attitude of the grown ups that were sat around, and I remember the appreciation I felt for what he was saying.*

Children were very receptive to the mood of adults (they are anyway) and to the propaganda messages bombarding the public during the War. One theme which did emerge during these discussions was the idea of the menacing nature of the German people, especially German soldiers. These were perceived as an advancing army, an invisible threatening cloud surrounding the town. The children dealt with their fears of invasion by employing the use of some pretty effective psychological defence mechanisms — Jerry, could be ridiculed, for example:

❖ *— Oh, we were given images all the time (of the German soldiers). He was called a Nazi and he was called a Jerry. As kids we related this to the Jerry that went under the bed, but I really don't know why he was called a Jerry, but I thought he had fallen to the level of being a Jerry under the bed.*

Or he could be objectified, made less than human.

❖ *— This man, he was a pretty young man, he was part of the Home Guard, and he came to school to give us this lecture of how, if there was a gas attack, how we had to lie flat on the floor, and he was telling us various things about what to do if they was bombing and everything, all the things that we really needed to know, if we found ourselves on our own in a bombed condition. He said at the end of it, 'are there any questions?' and this boy of about eight*

years of age said, 'yes, I've got a question?' and he said, 'what is
it?' He said, 'when you stick your bayonet into a Jerry, and it gets
stuck, do you have to twist it round like that to get it out?' What I
remember about this was that there was no little girls squealing, no
little boys went 'ugh.' We were all very interested in the answer.
Did they have to unscrew it or take it off? The only shocked face in
the room was his, the one who had been asked the question. I don't
think for one moment when he asked if anyone wanted to ask a
question that he would get one like that. He paused for a moment
and then he said, 'well I suppose you'd have to unscrew it,' but its
often made me think when I remember that how we were absolutely
fed on violence and hatred. I can remember really hating the
Germans, and I never for one moment thought about the horror of a
bayonet going into a human being — it was just a Jerry anyway,
and who was he?

Fear of the Jerries was one thing. Fear of being unable to feed your
family was for many women almost as worrying as the threat of invasion.
The storytellers could remember the food scarcities, the rationing and the
various strategies people used to get around these problems. 'Above board'
so to speak , people simply swapped tokens. Some storytellers spoke of
others they had known who had dealt with black -market goods (though
none admitted to having done such a thing themselves) 'Someone else'
always dealt with 'spivs' as one woman admitted.

❖ *Anyone who bought black-market goods was really looked*
down on, but people all denied doing it and yet the spivs (the
slang name for a person who supplies black market goods) were
doing really well (laughs) so someone must have been buying the
stuff, so you knew the spiv was selling his stuff to someone, but
you never knew who to.

But there were more 'honourable,' ways of ensuring that your family
did not go short other than dealing with a spiv.

❖ *— (Laughs) Oh, I remember they talked about Mrs Brown.*

'I don't understand it,' they would say, 'I'm sure she must be dealing with spivs, because every time she opens her cupboard it's full of food and, and chocolates, all these things.' People couldn't understand it, how she could have all this food when everything was so rationed ... and it was many years later, long after the war that they found out that — she was a very professional shoplifter ... (laughs) but, during the War, she was accused of doing something far worse than being a shoplifter, she was accused of dealing with black-market goods.

Things we now take for granted were much desired and, if you were lucky enough to get something of what you wanted, greatly treasured. Manners often went out of the window when news of the availability of some scarcity hit town.

❖ *— I remember oranges being scarce and I loved bananas, I really longed for bananas all through the War. I had a friend and her father was in Africa and he was allowed to send a parcel round Christmas, and one year he sent some pomegranates which I'd never heard of before, and I was given a banana and I absolutely loved it. Spanish onions, they were scarce, any onions in fact, and I remember them saying they'd got oranges at the greengrocers and everyone would run, and then they would all be arguing because some of them would go to the back of the queue and everyone would be saying, 'ey, you've had one.'*

But no matter how opportunistic rationing could make people, there was one occasion when everyone could be counted on to be generous. This was when a young soldier came from the war front to visit home.

❖ *I remember the good times and I remember the happiness when such and such a body's son would come home on leave. We all shared the joy, and everyone shared the sorrow. If a man came home and the family hadn't much in, people would actually go to that home with bits and bats of things to help them out, to help them make his homecoming a welcome one.*

It is little wonder that families made a fuss when a soldier came home to visit. The news of a family member being killed came all too often. The night Manchester was bombed was a turning point in the history of Bolton. The horrendous spectacle of a city aflame striking terror into the hearts of those who witnessed it, was to be the hallmark of an experience which I for one feel thankful to have missed. War was no longer an abstract 'thing' happening in another land far away, it was here, in Bolton, ever threatening to take the lives of civilians. Children as young as eight years old were to be given lectures in school from members of the Home Guard on how to survive in the event of a gas attack. Although the children instructed in this way did not fully understand the dangers of their situation (thankfully) who knows what psychological torment children might have suffered in their own private little world? How confusing it must have been for them. On the one hand adults were telling them they wouldn't get shot. On the other they were being instructed on what to do in the event of a gas attack. We worry nowadays about the possible harmful effects of violence on television, and yet less then fifty years ago, young children went to the local cinema to cheer at the spectacle of German soldiers being blown to pieces, brought to the local picture place by the war newsreels. And the problems did not end when the last bombs landed on Bolton and War came to an end. As we shall see in the next chapter, ordinary people were to carry on paying for the price of the War for many years afterwards.

CHAPTER EIGHT

THE PRICE OF A POPPY

❖ — *There were some nice young men went . . . it was a shame, it was terrible, all those nice young men gone.*

I cannot put myself in this story because I have never experienced anything so terrible as the events I will be describing here. Most of the young men I grew up with are still alive, now like me, respectable, married or divorced, parents and householders, living ordinary lives which we seldom consider as being fortunate or privileged. Only three of the people I grew up with have died at the time I write this book — and that was bad enough. There is something especially horrible about someone of your own age dying — it brings home to you your own mortality. But the young deceased I knew (I tell myself) were exceptions to the rule. Two died of cancer, the third, a young man in his twenties, was the victim of a road traffic accident. Apart from victims of accidental death, cancer, heart disease, we expect nowadays to live to a ripe old age of seventy plus — hence the sense of outrage when this does not happen.

We consider longevity to be a natural state of affairs these days. This was not the case however, for the women who took part in this study. For all of them, even the younger women in their late fifties, death has been very much a part of life. This chapter is concerned with the loss of life during the two Wars and the psychologically traumatised youths who were at least fortunate enough to have survived. One of the advantages of an oral history approach when conducting research is that it vividly captures the essence of individual and social experience, in particular the effects of war on ordinary people. We can read factual accounts of the great Wars in standard history books, the famous battles, the defeats and the victories. We can get the statistics of how many lives were lost, how many casualties etc. But all this we understand in abstract, objective terms — its hard to wrap a human being around a statistic. But when we hear people talk of loved ones lost at war and witness the personal sense of loss and regret in the voice of the storyteller we are faced with a heart-breaking realisation of what war really means.

War is heartbreaking. This statement is so true that it seems senseless to even bother saying it. Yet how many of us really think about this when we think of war? For those of us fortunate enough to have been spared direct experience of war, it is hard really very hard for us to understand. War is much crueller than an ordinary bereavement. This is terrible but at least it is final. People can begin the grieving process, reorganise their lives and start to live again. But the parents who said goodbye to sons, the young wives who kissed their husbands off to War, had no way of knowing if this would be a temporary or final goodbye.

> ❖ — *What saddened me was the telegraph boy, I knew that was very serious — the telegraph boy rode a bike, and more often than not he didn't come to say someone was missing he came to say that someone had died. I remember one particular family, well I remember a few families, but I remember the bike coming up St. Thomas Street and I remember everyone looking and they must have been in terrible shock because wives and mothers were stressed you know, waiting and fearing that it would stop at their door you know, and if it did, oh the horror on that persons face . . . oh, it, you really couldn't describe it you know, it was terrible.*

One reported response to the arrival of the telegraph boy was denial. This was perhaps more disturbing than acceptance of the death. It seems from the storytellers' accounts that many people simply refused to believe that their loved one had been killed. A normal response in early bereavement is shock, numbness and denial but for many people bereaved during the two Wars, this developmental stage in the grieving process was frozen, often suspended until the War had ended.

> ❖ *But those who did lose their men, I think it only hit them after the War, especially with the celebrations, and then people didn't accept that they were dead. That was very common, they felt that a mistake had been made, false identity, and then after the War they didn't come back. They'd be saying, 'I don't think he is dead, I think they will find him.'*

The lack of a body may have further complicated a bereaved person's ability to accept the death of a loved one. A body is not a person, but for those who knew the deceased it is the testimony of a life. In the event of a death most people need the presence of a body. This is why the laying out of a body is considered so important to nurses. For those nurses who lay out a person they have nursed this will be the last duty they will perform for the deceased and as such it is a way of paying tribute to that person. It may be that the body provides a way of paying respect to the person who had once lived there. It also provides tangible proof of the death itself. It is generally accepted that people suffer tremendous distress if the body of someone they love cannot be found and laid to rest. We hear of this all the time on the media. Heartbroken parents of murdered children for example, appeal to their child's killer to name the place where the body can be found. There is probably much more to such behaviour then the need to give the deceased a decent burial. There is much ritual and symbolism attached to a funeral and this may provide some psychological millstone in the grieving process. Therefore, it may well be the case that we need the body of someone we have lost in order to accept the death. When we consider how huge death is, bigger than we can comprehend, then it is little wonder that we need concrete evidence before many of us could accept the death of someone we love and give up all hope that a mistake had been made. It was the opinion of several of the storytellers, that the lack of a body did complicate the grieving process for many people.

Chris — *Do you think that not having a body made things worse?*

❖ *Not having a body? Yes, I do, you see there was nothing, no way of grasping it, and another thing was, 'missing presumed killed', or 'missing in action', and then sometimes, it would be months and months after, they'd get a letter to notify them that they had been taken prisoner, and then even worse, to be notified that they'd died in a prison camp.*

The limitations of language leave us incapable of describing the psychological trauma people suffered at times such as this. How, in view of all this, have we escaped having a generation of older people who are so mentally crushed that they are unable to live any kind of normal life at all? Before I started the interviews for this study, I accepted in some vague way that people lost loved ones in the event of a war and of course I thought about how sad this must have been. But I had never thought for a moment of the terrible uncertainty people had to live with, of not knowing if a loved one had died or not — to be told a loved one was presumed dead, then found, then dead again. And people frequently experienced not one loss or even two. There were some people who had lost several family members in one stroke during a battle or a bombing.

❖ *There were quite a few lads I knew that was killed in the War. Some were in the army and others were in the navy, but I personally had three cousins killed all in one go, it was three brothers all got killed at Dunkirk.*

Some relatives waiting at home however, accepted that they would almost certainly lose someone. For individuals such as this the arrival of the telegraph boy was just a matter of time. But some could be pleasantly surprised.

❖ *Now this happened to a woman who lived next door to us, and she had a husband and three sons away at War, and they were all in the navy, and they had all been involved in a sea battle, and although they were all in different ships, they were all involved in the same battle and I think that out of that there was one missing, but they did find him, and I remember them coming with that news and she just felt that it was too good to be true, that she could have a husband who would come out of it and her sons, she didn't think that she would have them all, but she did, she was very lucky.*

The majority of women were at home, working and waiting. But some women did go to War and like the men, lost their lives. One of the storytellers reported that a greater percentage of married women went to work in the mills during the Second World War because there was a shortage of single women. Many single women apparently, signed up and went to War.

❖ — *Do you think the War (the second) had anything to do with more married women going into the mill?*

❖ *Oh, well, they had because a lot of these young uns, they joined up and went in the waffs, and the sea cadets. There really was a shortage (of single women) because they all joined up. There was a lot went in the card room. We had four (in the spinning room) and they were in the St. John's Ambulance, so they had to go to War.*

One of the women interviewed told of losing a friend, a young woman.

❖ *I even know some (women) who got killed in the ATS, the women's army. One, she was on the search lights and this stray thing came and hit her, and that was it, during a raid.*

The heartbreak of war did not end with the death of someone you loved. Those who survived the War came back greatly changed by the War. For married couples hoping to rebuild their relationship, this was further complicated by the fact that the women had also changed. Married couples were strangers to each other. People do change over the years. But it seems the experiences of War had intensified change and these changes in both men and women for a variety of reasons. Some women had simply fallen in love with someone else while their husbands were away. Although this was greatly frowned upon, it was probably quite common. Four of the storytellers mentioned it, which is quite a large percentage in such a small sample.

❖ *I remember when they came back after the War, and I remember as a child someone saying, 'I wonder how she'll go on with that spiv.' A spiv was a person who had managed to keep out of the War. There were some who had a genuine reason for keeping out of the War, that wasn't a spiv. A spiv made money selling black-market stuff and they were often womanisers as well.*

It is understandable that people would disapprove of a married woman going out with someone else while her husband was away at War. It is equally understandable that some wives would be tempted to do so. The women were under a great deal of stress. They probably felt lonely and unsure of whether their husbands were still alive. It is little wonder in such circumstances that some women turned to someone else for love and affection. Some wives however, had grown accustomed to living alone and simply liked the independence. This complicated matters even further. Husbands and wives were not the only family members to experience difficulties. Children also found it difficult to build relationships with fathers who were strangers to them.

❖ *I always think that the first twelve months of marriage are the worst, because you are just getting used to one another, and it was difficult again, when he came home from the War, because I'd got used to having my children on my own, and my youngest son never ever got used to my husband, and I always blamed it on the War. They were all right but he was never as close to him as my eldest son because my eldest son remembered him, you see, the youngest didn't remember him.*

Women provided each other with tremendous support during the War years. The home had become more than ever before, a woman's place, despite the fact that more married women worked. It is possible that some of the men felt threatened by the solidarity which had developed between women during the War years.

❖ *It's a funny thing, but War kind of brings people together, you know, everybody pulled together and helped each other. Well, you had to, it was a case of survival, I had a next door neighbour and she was an absolutely wonderful friend to me, and we used to emulsion the walls, distempering them they called it, decorating and they used to stipple it with a sponge, do it a different colour to make a pattern on the paper, and we used to do the garden as best we could.*

One way in which relationships are established is for couples to engage in a process of disclosure — telling our secrets to a loved one. Two of the women interviewed for this study reported that their husbands confessed to having visited a brothel while abroad.

❖ *And he once told me when he came home that he'd been in a brothel and he said that it was absolutely awful, he'd been with his mates you know, they thought they'd have a bash, you know, and he said it was horrible . . . well, sex isn't love, is it?*

In each of the brothel stories the husband assured his wife that the experience was horrible. So the brothel story may have served a function other than the obvious one of relieving feelings of guilt. The confession provided an opportunity to share a secret with the wife, a way of re-establishing the relationship by sharing some intimacy. The brothel stories do reflect a double standard of sexual behaviour for men and women. There were no stories of wives telling their husbands of any extra marital affairs they might have had. But the confessions do suggest that the young couple were rebuilding their relationships, starting from scratch, rather then simply picking up where they had left off.

For some couples, the quality of the marriage improved after the War. The married couple had learned to value their relationship all the more because of their enforced separation. One storyteller told of a man she had known who had neglected his family terribly prior to the War, spending

most of his time and money in the pub. This man was completely re-
formed because of his War experiences and he came back anxious to make
a success of family life.

Other women had taken up jobs outside the home, especially in the
local mills which had encouraged married women into employment
because of the shortage of single women during the War. It seems that
this caused problems in some marriages. There were husbands who did
not want their wives to continue working. But the wives enjoyed the
company and financial independence the mills offered and were very
reluctant to give up their jobs. Other men felt tormented, suspecting that
their wives may have been unfaithful while they had been away. The
combination of these various problems led to some terrible marital problems for many families. The storyteller below gives a graphic account how
psychologically crippled some men were after the War, causing problems
for the whole family.

> ❖ *Unbearable, (the men) they couldn't settle, you couldn't seem*
> *to do anything right for them, they soon lost their tempers and*
> *called you all the names under the sun, it took a good two or*
> *three years for some of them to get back to normal . . . it was very*
> *hard on their wives, and the kiddies as well, because the kiddies*
> *wondered what was wrong, they couldn't understand it and the*
> *wives were so fed up they'd just give in to it, and some of them*
> *were terrible . . . On the street I lived, one came home, he*
> *couldn't settle, so he used to beat her up, he accused her of going*
> *with men, he said the cotton mills were to blame, that cotton*
> *workers were all the same. She ended up divorcing him, and*
> *eventually he had to go into a mental hospital, because the War*
> *had turned him like that, but some of them were like that about*
> *the mills, we were the lowest of the low.*

It is clear from the account given above that the husband was suffering
psychological problems of some sort, due to his experiences of the War.
But there seem to have been two other issues in this case which may have

added to the strain on the couple's marriage. The first was the husband's belief that his wife had been unfaithful to him despite the fact that there appears to have been no evidence at all to suggest that she had. The second was that the husband feared the independence his wife enjoyed due to her job in the local mill. This latter theme came up quite a lot in the interviews and it seems that one weapon used by some men to persuade their wives to give up their jobs was to foster the idea that such employment had a corrupting effect. So the idea was promoted that mill workers were (to use the storytellers terminology) 'the lowest of the low.' This is interesting by the late sixties the stereotype of the 'common,' mill worker had become quite strong. But it is clear that this negative stereotype was quite a recent development in the history of the mills.

The older women in the study made it clear that mill had once been a respected occupation for which any worker could feel proud. It is possible that the negative image of mill worker may have evolved just after the War. At this time wives were being persuaded by husbands and other authorities to return to the home — somewhat unsuccessfully it would seem from these accounts. The money wives earned in the mills may have threatened the fathers' traditional positions of power in the family. It is clear from the older women's accounts that there was nothing new about married women working in the mills. But after the Second World War a new ideology appeared which promoted the nuclear family as the ideal more than ever before. Prior to the War, it is clear that the husband had been considered the head of the household; this was the case even when the husband was unemployed. But for whatever reason, it seems from the interviews in this study that men felt very vulnerable once they returned from the War and they perceived a need to reclaim their 'threatened' place as family head. This perceived threat seems to have been much greater after the Second World War than after the First.

It is difficult to explain why such a difference should exist. It may be that the events of War left men feeling so utterly powerless that there was a need to reclaim at least some of the control in their lives, at least in their own homes. But this does not explain why the Second World War seemed to have a much greater psychological effect than the First. It is possible of course, that there was no difference. Men may have been difficult to live with after both Wars, but for some reason the older women did not mention such problems in connection with the First World War. The older women had experienced the First World War as children. Therefore, they may not have sensed the possibility that their parents were experiencing marital problems. Or maybe the memories of the problems they had experienced after the Second World War blocked out memories of the First.

It seems from the majority of the stories told at the interviews, that wives tried very hard to be understanding and patient with their husbands. Several of them showed deep compassion when discussing what things must have been like for their husbands fighting in the War. The storyteller quoted below spent a long time during her interview, trying to imagine and describe the horrors her husband must have experienced and of how the attitudes of the men had changed towards War, many thinking it was a waste of time.

> ❖ — *They'd seen people killed, they'd seen their mates killed, my husband told me this day they had this German attack, and he said his mate who was next to him during this attack, by the time it was finished he was dead. They were seeing their friends blown to pieces right in front of them. My husband told me about that, so it must have definitely affected them, it can't do anything else but affect them can it? . . . I think so, war's just a waste of time, I think most people, especially the men thought it was, and I think that now.*

Some men had the ordeal of the prisoner of war to recover from as well. Some had to live like animals in order to survive.

> ❖ *But the prisoner who survived who came back at the end of the War, said that the ones who survived were the ones who would eat anything, anything whatsoever; the ones who didn't survive were the ones who couldn't eat grass, insects, anything they could get their hands on you know?*

It wasn't just within their marriages that men had difficulties. Problems of adjustment spilled into other areas of their lives as well, such as their jobs. Those who had been to War did at least have the chance of work. Those who had stayed, to work in munitions for example, were heavily discriminated against after the War.

> ❖ *When they came back (after working on the munitions) they couldn't get a job. They'd say, 'have you been in the munitions,' and if you said that you'd been in the munitions they'd say 'sorry, we don't want none,' ... well, they knew you'd not been in the War you see. A lot went in the munitions because they knew they'd not have to go in the War, but when you went for a job like after, there was no way anyone would employ you. People were angry that they'd lost husbands, sons and more, so when they saw these who' managed to get out of it, you see, so that were it.*

Such discrimination may seem very unjust, but who knows how any of us might feel about losing someone we love and of how this might make us respond? This does not, of course, condone such discrimination, but when we try to put ourselves in the place of those who experienced the Wars, it does help us to at least understand such feelings. There is a saying that war brings out the best in people, but it seems from this study that it can bring out the worst as well.

Every year the poppies fall. Floating at first in uniform fashion, they gradually lose each other. Like a startled flock of birds, they spin off in various directions. Where — nowhere. Young enthusiastic hope, scattered and lost forever. A generation turned to dust. Perhaps the poppy's real meaning does not just refer to the physical death of thousands of young men, but also another sort of death, the loss of a stable, happy, well-adjusted life for millions of families — which in many cases proved permanent. The poppy stands for the lost lives, the lost years and the lost possibilities.

> ❖ *Its very hard to think about, and you know, when I think about all the young men who were killed, such young men you*

know, losing their lives, and I sometimes think, well was it worth it you know, I mean, who thinks about them now, all those young lads, its such a shame.

CHAPTER NINE

THE COTTON PROCESS

This final chapter gives the reader a simplified account of the cotton process and is provided as a reference so that some of the things said by the contributors will make better sense. The information which was required to write this section of the book was provided partly by the storytellers and partly by an information leaflet produced by the International Institute for Cotton. The chapter should not be considered as the work of a textile 'expert' which I am not, and do not make any claims to be, but rather a very basic account of the process, so that the stories will hopefully be more meaningful.

The cotton process in the mills was to begin with the delivery of the raw cotton which needed to be cleaned (this process being completed by the 'scutching machine') and separated from the waste products it carried. All the raw cotton was brought to the scutching hole which was usually based on the first floor. Some of the storytellers spoke of a large room where the cotton was stored and from the descriptions they gave it would seem that they may have been referring to the scutching hole.

❖ *Dinner hour was really great for the young ones. We would get together and sit around the mill lodge and we'd joke about and talk and generally just lark about, and sometimes (and this was fantastic) we'd sneak into the rooms were they kept all the cotton wool and throw ourselves around in the cotton and we'd be laughing our heads off and because of the amount of noise we*

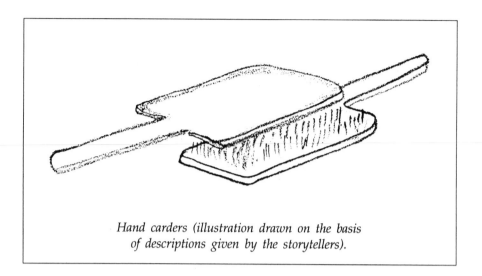

*Hand carders (illustration drawn on the basis
of descriptions given by the storytellers).*

*were making, sooner or later a strict voice would come and shout
'what's going on?' at which we would become completely silent'.*

Another storyteller, whose job when she first started in the mills was
to take waste cotton back to the scutching hole, spoke of the impressive
machinery.

❖ *'I loved this job because I could walk all over the two mills
with freedom. My journey would take me to the scutching hole
where two handsome men used to feed the raw cotton into the
scutcher. The scutcher separated the waste from the pure and
clean cotton, that was stored in large compartments, it was a
room full of cotton wool. I would call into the engine room to
give the men in there clean cleaning cloths. The machine they
worked on, I used to really marvel at, it really was a magnificent
thing with its engine turning this great wheel. It had this
gigantic shining arm. It never failed to fill me with awe at its
sheer beauty and the men who worked the engine oiled and
greased it with tender loving care.*

Outside there was a dock where lorries delivered bunches of tightly packed cotton called 'bales'. There were usually two men who worked the scutching machines with possibly one labourer to fetch and carry the bales. Once the raw cotton had been released from the tightly packed bales, it would enter the scutching machine, often called a 'breaker', 'blower' or 'opener'. This machine broke up the fluffy balls of cotton and blew them aloft so that the cotton fibres were separated from what was known as the 'shoddy', a grey mass of fluffy stuff made up of poorer quality cotton and anything else which could have been picked up during the picking from the cotton fields, such as dirt, grit, even the remains of some wildlife habitat — all this waste would fall to the bottom of the machine where it could be removed. When all the foreign bodies were removed from the 'shoddy' I was told by the storytellers that it would be sent to mills which dealt with the making of less fine produce such as floor cloths, cleaning cloths and some types of curtains.

When the raw cotton had been blown and the shoddy separated, it then went to the card room. In the few remaining mills that exist today much of the processing has been abbreviated and one machine can do the work of what might have been done by three in the past. The stories of the women who took part in this study, tell of how the work was done many years ago when more workers were needed.

Carding

At the time of which the storytellers were speaking (the time span between the twenties and late sixties) the cotton would first be put on the carding machine which would compact and flatten it prior to passing it onto cylinders. At this stage it would look like thick course cotton wool (referred to as a 'lap'). This cylinder, or large roller was covered with fine wire points and which rotated beneath a canopy, also covered with fine teeth. The action of these two cylinders converted the tufts of cotton into a flat web of fibres which was then gathered together into a rope about 25 mm in diameter called a 'sliver' which wound from the carding machine into a tall can for storage or transportation.

The next stage was to process the sliver through a draw frame. This machine blended the different kinds of cotton together to produce an even mixture and progressively pulled the strands into thinner, stronger yarn, this process was called 'parallelising' the fibres. Next, the cotton was passed through a speed frame which contained several pairs of rollers which reduced the slivers to 'rovings' (finer yarn which was about 5mm in diameter) which were then wound onto large bobbins ready for spinning.

Prior to the growth of the industrial revolution, in the cottage industry, the process of preparing the cotton for spinning (later known as carding) was done by hand. The worker held in each hand an instrument consisting of two cards, layered with wire teeth on each inner side. A layer of cotton tufts would be drawn across the lower card and the upper card would be drawn across it.

Although on a very small scale, this simple process would clean and comb the cotton and lay the fibres into a delicate web, with the carding machines, it would then be rolled by hand into a sausage like shape, so that it could then be drawn, again by hand onto the spinning machine.

Spinning

Different thicknesses of yarn produce different qualities of fabric. Spinning reduced the rovings of fibres into the final thickness of yarn required (this was referred to as the 'count' of the yarn) and secured them in place by giving them a final twist. This process has been done by hand since ancient times but was speeded up with the invention of spinning machines used in the cottage industries of the 18th century. The spinning machine was limited to the production of only one yarn at a time, but in the 19th century invention of machines such as the 'Spinning Mule' (invented by Samuel Crompton) the 'Spinning Jenny' and the 'Water Frame' allowed dozens of yarn to be spun simultaneously and at much greater speed. Mule spinning was remembered by many of the storytellers and this was a mans occupation *(see discussion in chapter six).*

> ❖ *I ended up with the Mule spinners, now. These were a special breed of men. They paced the floor in their bare feet between these huge moving monsters (the machines) backwards and*

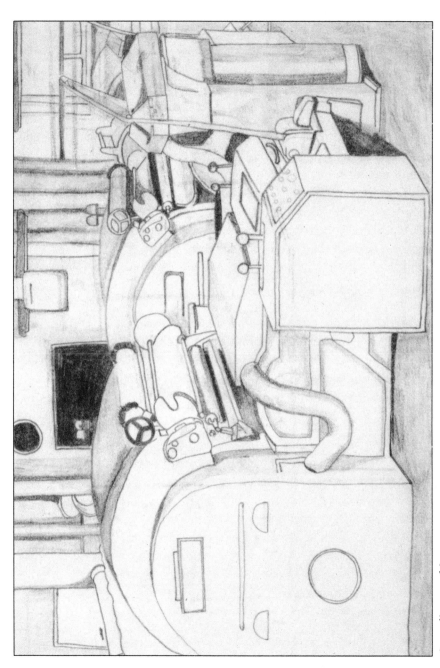

A carding machine

forwards, stretching and twisting the yarn ready for the winder, I would hand over the 'bad ends' (these were parts of the yarn which had remained fluffy and were removed) The ends were taken back to make the spinners feel ashamed because they had failed to remove the "bad ends" before the yarn got to the winder.

Ring spinning *(which is also referred to in chapter six)* was developed from Richard Arkwright's Water Frame, developed about 1769. Ring spinning was to be a woman's occupation.

By the time the cotton arrived at the spinning room the 'rovings' would be twisted. This was much the same as it had been twisted in the cottage industries, the cotton being twisted as it spun and caught the end of the spindle as it was made into bobbins of thread now suitable to be woven. In the spinning process the rovings would pass between rollers, drawing it out to a greater length. Having passed through the rollers it would be guided by a 'traveller'. The traveller spun around the ring to make an even bobbin ready to be taken to the winding rooms. The process of spinning became increasingly rapid as the years passed and in addition to the spinner's working on them, teams of 'doffers' would walk around the machines taking off empty bobbins and replacing these with full ones (some storytellers referred to this task as 'setting on').

❖ *There was four in a team of doffers and there was two on each side of the machine, one started in the middle and another started at the end. As soon as the bobbins were full, the machine would come to a stop and you had to take the full ones off, and put them in a can which you had in front of you which rested on a sliding rail. There were two sliding rails and a can which was just above your knee, in fact you could move it with your knee. There were two compartments, one would hold the empty bobbins, which you would take in your hand; you would remove one with one hand and slip the new bobbin on with the other. You had to be very, very quick. The average time for a machine being doffed was about five minutes with a good team, but you had to be with a good team and if you were lucky you got a rest in between.*

Fig Three: A Spinning Machine

Doffing was usually one of the first jobs young people entering the mill were assigned to. In addition to this work, the young workers were often given little errands and tasks to do by the spinners.

❖ *At ten o' clock (in the morning) you could go down to the cellars to make a pot of tea. They would send a doffer, so we were running up and down stairs bringing them pots of tea.*

This additional task of brewing up during the morning break would mean that the young doffers would be running up and down two or three flights of stairs, in addition to all the exercise they would get walking around the machines changing bobbins — little wonder that they were able to burn off all the calories provided in their mothers home cooked meals *(see chapter five)*.

Winding

Basically, winding was a process which prepared the yarn for crealing, the first stage of weaving the fabric. There were many kinds of winding. Some winding machines produced yarn ready for 'doubling'. Doubling consisted of doubling two ends or threads in order to make them stronger. There were also 'perm winders' who made a small cob which would fit onto a shuttle for the weaver. Cob winders made 'cheeses'*(see fig. six)*. Usually two cobs were wound into a cheese shaped spool. This would go into the doublers and they were doubled up once more from the cheeses onto a bobbin passing through rollers and liquid as it did so.

These cheeses went to the bottle winders, thus called because when wound they were shaped like bottles. Then there were gas winders. During the gas winding process the thread would pass through a small gas flame which burned off any furry fibres surrounding the thread. This thread was used for the weaving of very fine materials. In the process of all types of winding the yarn would go through the clearers which allowed all the perfectly spun yarn through but stopped any imperfect thread from going through. This was because without the perfect twist in the thread, it would be more fluffy, more like a roving than spun yarn. These were called 'bad ends' and were a great source of frustration to the winder if the thread contained too many because she would be working harder for less money. Most winding was piece work, in other words, the workers were paid according to how much they produced. Unfortunately the yarn had to have a lot of bad ends indeed before the workers were given any allowance for them. Skips from the ring room, filled with cops or bobbins were placed at the back of the winder and these were packed on shelves above or below the worker, depending on the type of frame on which they worked. Hopefully for the worker, the ends would be running well so that this job could be done without any interruptions in the processing — interruptions cost the worker money so that speed and deftness were crucial.

If the thread did break then it was the job of the winder to 'piece up' (knot the threads back together) so that the process of winding could continue. In the early days of the cotton industry this piecing up was done by hand using a pair of scissors. Later, hand instruments called 'knotters' were introduced which knotted the threads together automatically at the flick of a switch. *Page 135* gives the reader an illustration of an electric winding machine.

Crealing

This was the first stage of the weaving process whereby the threads which would make up the length of the cloth (known as the 'warp') would be wound onto a large roller called a beam.

Weaving

Weaving was the final stage in which the yarn was converted into cloth. Once the beam containing the warp was full it was transferred to a weaving machine, or 'loom'. Weaving involves interlocking a 'weft' (using an instrument called a 'shuttle') yarn through the 'warp', from edge to edge across the width of the cloth. Weaving, as with all other processes in the mill, became faster and faster as the years passed. The speed at which the weaving was completed depended on the time it took for the 'shuttle' to move back and forth across the fabric (this is referred to as the 'picking rate'). Only one weaver was interviewed in this study and she told me that she loved the work.

The weaving process demanded that the worker had lots of light so that they could see the patterns created by the yarn clearly and thus detect any defects in the cloth. Because of this (I was told by the storytellers) weaving sheds had a characteristic, 'zig-zag' type of a roof which was partly glazed to allow as much sun into the room as possible and the ceilings were also painted white.

Once the weaving of the fabric had been completed the fabric would go through further processing in order to finish it (cleaning the cloth to remove any natural waxes and to remove any stains) and to bleach it to an even whiteness. Finally the cloth may be coloured by dying or patterned by printing. Additional finishings may be added to make the cloth flame proof or waterproof.

An Electric Winding Machine